PAY IT FORWARD

Published by CelebrityPress®, Orlando, FL.

CelebrityPress® is a registered trademark.

Printed in the United States of America.

ISBN: 978-1-7334176-6-2
LCCN: 2020913296

This publication is designed to provide accurate and authoritative information with regard to the subject matter covered. It is sold with the understanding that the publisher is not engaged in rendering legal, accounting, or other professional advice. If legal advice or other expert assistance is required, the services of a competent professional should be sought. The opinions expressed by the authors in this book are not endorsed by CelebrityPress® and are the sole responsibility of the author rendering the opinion.

Most CelebrityPress® titles are available at special quantity discounts for bulk purchases for sales promotions, premiums, fundraising, and educational use. Special versions or book excerpts can also be created to fit specific needs.

For more information, please write:
CelebrityPress®
520 N. Orlando Ave, #2
Winter Park, FL 32789
or call 1.877.261.4930

Visit us online at: www.CelebrityPressPublishing.com

CelebrityPress®
Winter Park, Florida

CONTENTS

CHAPTER 1

CREATE YOUR OWN FUTURE

BY BRIAN TRACY

You will become as small as your controlling desire;
or as great as your dominant aspiration.
~ James Allen

In more than 3300 studies of leaders conducted over the years, there is a special quality that stands out, one quality that all great leaders have in common. It is the quality of vision. Leaders have vision. Non-leaders do not.

Earlier, I said that the most important discovery in all of human history is that, "You become what you think about – most of the time." What is it then that leaders think about, most of the time? And the answer is that leaders think about the future and where they are going, and what they can do to get there.

Non-leaders, on the other hand, think about the present, and the pleasures and problems of the moment. They think and worry about the past, and what has happened that cannot be changed.

THINK ABOUT THE FUTURE

We call this leadership quality **"Future-Orientation."** Leaders think about the future and what they want to accomplish, and where they want to arrive sometime down the road. Leaders think about what they want, and what can be done to achieve it. The good news is that, when you begin to think about your future as well, you begin to think like a *leader*, and you will soon get the same results that leaders get.

Dr. Edward Banfield of Harvard concluded, after more than 50 years of research, that "long-time perspective" was the most important determinant of financial and personal success in life. Banfield defined long-time perspective as the "ability to think several years into the future while making decisions in the present." This is one of the most important discoveries ever made. Just think! The further you think into the future, the better decisions you will make in the present to assure that that future becomes a reality.

BECOME A MILLIONAIRE

For example, if you save $100 per month from the age of 20 to the age of 65, and you invested that money in a mutual fund earning an average of 10% per annum over time, you would be worth more than $1,118,000 dollars when you retired.

Anyone who really wanted to could save $100 per month, if he or she had a long enough time perspective. What this means is that every single person starting work today can become a millionaire over time if they begin early enough, save consistently enough, and hold to their long-term vision of financial independence.

CREATE A FIVE-YEAR FANTASY

In personal strategic planning, you should begin with a long-term view of your life, as well. You should begin by practicing *idealization* in everything you do. In the process of idealization, you create a *five-year fantasy* for yourself, and begin thinking about what your life would look like in five years if it were perfect in every respect.

The biggest single obstacle to setting goals is "self-limiting beliefs." These are areas where you believe yourself to be limited in some way. You may believe yourself to be inadequate or inferior in areas such as intelligence, ability, talent, creativity, personality or something else. As a result, you sell yourself short. By underestimating yourself, you set either no goals, or low goals that are far below what you are truly capable of accomplishing.

IMAGINE NO LIMITATIONS

By combining *idealization* and *future-orientation*, you cancel or neutralize this process of self-limitation. You imagine for the moment that you have **no limitations** at all. You imagine that you have all the time, talents and abilities you could ever require to achieve any goal you could set for yourself. No matter where you are in life, you imagine that you have all the friends, contacts and relationships you need to open every door and achieve anything you could really want. You imagine that you have no limitations whatsoever on what you could be, have or do in the pursuit of the goals that are really important to you.

PRACTICE BLUE SKY THINKING

In Charles Garfield's studies of "Peak Performers," he made an interesting discovery. He analyzed men and women who had achieved only average results at work for many years, but who suddenly exploded into great success and accomplishment. He found that at the "take-off point," every one of them began engaging in what he called "Blue Sky Thinking."

In blue-sky thinking, you imagine that all things are possible for you, just like looking up into a clear blue sky, with no limits. You project forward several years and imagine that your life were perfect in every respect sometime in the future. You then look back to where you are today and ask yourself this question: "What would have to have happened, for me to have created my perfect future?"

You then come back to where you are in the present in your own mind, and you ask, "What would have to happen from this point forward for me to achieve all my goals sometime in the future?"

REFUSE TO COMPROMISE YOUR DREAMS

When you practice idealization and future-orientation, you make no compromises with your dreams and visions for yourself and your future. You don't settle for smaller goals or half successes. Instead, you "dream big dreams" and project forward mentally as though you are one of the most powerful people in the universe. You create your perfect future. You decide what you really want, before you come back to the present moment and deal with what is possible for you within your current situation.

Start with your business and career. Imagine that your work life was perfect five years from now. Answer these questions:

- What would it look like?
- What would you be doing?
- Where would you be doing it?
- Who would you be working with?
- What level of responsibility would you have?
- What kind of skills and abilities would you have?
- What kind of goals would you be accomplishing?
- What level of status would you have in your field?

PRACTICE NO LIMIT THINKING

When you answer these questions, imagine that you have no limits. Imagine that everything is possible for you. Peter Drucker once said, *"We greatly overestimate what we can accomplish in one year. But we greatly underestimate what we can accomplish in five years."* Don't let this happen to you.

Now, idealize your perfect financial life sometime in the future:

- How much do you want to be earning five years from today?
- What sort of lifestyle do you want to have?
- What kind of home do you want to live in?
- What kind of car do you want to drive?
- What kind of material luxuries do you want to provide for yourself and your family?
- How much do you want to have in the bank?
- How much do you want to be saving and investing each month and each year?
- How much do you want to be worth when you retire?

Imagine that you have a "magic slate." You can write down anything you want. You can erase anything that may have happened in the past, and create whatever picture you desire for your future. You can clean the slate at any time and start over. You have no limits.

IMAGINE YOUR PERFECT FAMILY LIFE

Look at your family and relationships today, and project five years into the future:

If your family life were perfect five years from now, what would it look like?

- Who would you be with?
- Who would you no longer be with?
- Where and how would you be living?

- What kind of living standards would you have?
- What kind of relationships would you have with the most important people in your life, five years from now, if everything were perfect in every respect?

When you fantasize and imagine your perfect future, the only question you ask is, *"How?"* This is the most powerful question of all. Asking it repeatedly stimulates your creativity and triggers ideas to help you accomplish your goals. Unsuccessful people always wonder whether or not a particular goal is possible. High achievers on the other hand only ask the question, **"How?"** They then set to work to find ways to make their visions and goals into realities.

<u>IDEAL HEALTH AND FITNESS</u>

Review your levels of health and fitness in every area:

- If you were a perfect physical specimen five years from now, how would you look, feel and appear?
- What would be your ideal weight?
- How much would you exercise each week?
- What would be your overall level of health?
- What changes would you have to start making today in your diet, exercise routines and health habits to enjoy superb physical health sometime in the future?

You then imagine that you are an important and influential person, a "player" in your community. You are making a significant contribution to the world around you. You are making a difference with your life and in the lives of other people. If your social and community status and involvement were ideal:

- What would you be doing?
- What organizations would you expect to be working with or contributing to?
- What are the causes that you strongly believe in and support, and how could you become more involved in those areas?

JUST DO IT!

The primary difference between high achievers and low achievers is **"action-orientation."** Men and women who accomplish tremendous things in life are intensely action oriented. They are moving all the time. They are always busy. If they have an idea, they take action on it immediately.

On the other hand, low achievers and non-achievers are full of good intentions, but they always have an excuse for not taking action today. It is well said that, *"the road to hell is paved with good intentions."*

Examine yourself in terms of your personal inventory of skills, knowledge, talent, education and ability. If you were developed to the highest level possible for you (and there is virtually no limit), answer these questions:

- What additional knowledge and skills would you have acquired five years from now?
- In what areas would you be recognized as absolutely excellent in what you do?
- What would you be doing each day in order to develop the knowledge and skills you need to be one of the top performers in your field sometime in the future?

Once you have answered these questions, the only question you ask is:

- "How?" – How do you attain the skills and expertise you will require to lead your field in the years ahead?

17

DESIGN YOUR PERFECT CALENDAR

Especially, decide how you would like to live, day-in and day-out, your ideal lifestyle. Design your perfect calendar, from January 1st to December 31st:

- What would you like to do on your weekends and vacations?
- How much time would you like to take off each week, month and year?
- Where would you like to go?
- How would you organize your year if you had no limitations, and complete control over your time?

In the Bible it says, *"Where there is no vision, the people perish."* What this means is that, if you lack an exciting vision for your future, you will "perish" inside in terms of lacking motivation and enthusiasm for what you are doing. But the reverse of this is that, with an exciting future vision, you will be continuously motivated and stimulated every day to take the actions necessary to make your ideal vision a reality.

THE KEY TO HAPPINESS

You remember that, *"Happiness is the progressive realization of a worthy ideal."* When you have clear, exciting goals and ideals, you will feel happier about yourself and your world. You will be more positive and optimistic. You will be more cheerful and enthusiastic. You will feel *internally* motivated to get up and get going every morning, because every step you are taking will be moving you in the direction of something that is important to you.

Resolve to think about your ideal future most of the time. Remember, the very best days of your life lie ahead. The happiest moments you will ever experience are still to come. The highest income you will ever earn is going to materialize in the months and years ahead. The future is going to be better than anything that may have happened in your past. There are no limits.

The clearer you can be about your long term future, the more rapidly you will attract people and circumstances into your life to help make that future a reality. The greater clarity you have about who you are and what you want, the more you will achieve and the faster you will achieve it in every area of your life.

CREATE YOUR OWN FUTURE:

Imagine that there is a solution to every problem, a way to overcome every limitation, and no limit on your achieving every goal you can set for yourself. What would you do differently?

Practice "back from the future thinking." Project forward five years and look back to the present.

- What would have to have happened for your world to be ideal?

Imagine your financial life were perfect in every way.

- How much would you be earning?
- How much would you be worth?
- What steps could you take, starting today, to make these goals a reality?

Imagine your family and personal life was perfect.

- What would it look like?
- What should you start doing more of, or less of, starting today?

Plan your perfect calendar. Design your year from January to December as if you had no limitations.

- What would you change, starting today?

Imagine that your levels of health and fitness were perfect in every way.

What could you do, starting today, to make your vision for yourself into a reality?

19

About Brian

Brian Tracy is one of the top business experts and trainers in the world. He has taught more than 5,000,000 salespeople in 80 countries.

Brain is the President of Brian Tracy International, committed to teaching ambitious individuals how to rapidly increase their sales and personal incomes.

CHAPTER 2

YOU WILL NEVER BE THE SAME AGAIN

BY RINO SOLBERG
Chairman/Founder - Better Globe Group

I remember it, like if it was yesterday, the first time I watched the movie "Pay It Forward" with Kevin Spacey and Helen Hunt, it really got me thinking, and it changed my life in many more ways than one. At that time, I really wanted to do something different in my life, after being an international serial entrepreneur for over 40 years. In 1991, my wife, Julie Solberg, and I started an NGO called Child Africa. I had never experienced such happiness like on each occasion when we managed to find a sponsor for a child, so the child could go to school, to thereby secure the child's future. Both the child and the parents or guardians were so happy that it really overwhelmed me.

Fifteen years later, I decided to take on my last goal, which was planned to go on for the rest of my life and beyond: "To eradicate poverty and corruption in Africa." I knew I could never finish it in my lifetime, but I wanted to find ways to make it happen in a sustainable way, so the work could go on forever. Then, when I saw the above movie, I got many new ideas on how to make this happen.

The concept from the movie was that if I did something good for one or more people, they would be so happy that they also would "pay it forward" to others; this really grabbed my attention. It was actually the same thing I had done too, without thinking about it—when I told people I met about all the pleasure we got from sponsoring children in Africa, and they did the same. In fact, that gave me double happiness, by knowing that the child would get a better life, and to hear how much the sponsors themselves became happy because of being able to help too. That was proof that the principle worked with one area, now we just had to find more areas, one way or another, to "pay it forward," which we managed to do. So, let me tell you about it, and maybe it could help you too.

MAKING MONEY BY DOING GOOD

I knew that my goal; *"To eradicate poverty and corruption in Africa"* in a sustainable way could never be done by charity alone; it could only be done using business principles in a "social entrepreneurship" way, where everyone made money in the process. When I investigated who the poor people were, which we were going to eradicate poverty for in Africa, I found out that approximately 70% of Africans were small-hold farmers, with little or no education at all. Therefore, I had to find a money-making "product," which could give poor and mostly uneducated farmers, a possible income over time.

The answer was to plant high-quality mahogany trees, which took us two years just to find the right tree after I had started a company called Better Globe Forestry, Ltd in Kenya in 2004. However, I clearly understood that it would take both time and money to try out a model that worked.

However, little did I know that it should take us the next 13 years in a pilot project to make it happen. Despite the entire struggle over these years, we made it, and now we have a proven method for eradication of poverty and corruption in Africa and making a profit for participants at the same time. In 2015, the company even was awarded the "Taxpayers award" for small and medium-sized companies, handed out by the President of Kenya. Better Globe Forestry Ltd is today the most respected forestry company in Kenya, mostly thanks to my Managing Director and partner, Jean-Paul Deprins, who has been in charge since the beginning. He leads a great team of foresters and other managers, who all have taken on our vision. We now feel that we are ready to take the message to the world. However, this was the three-pronged approach we finally decided on:

1. <u>Massive Tree Planting (for Profit)</u>

Without massive forestation in Africa in the next 50 years, all land suitable for farming will probably be gone, and consequently, the farmers too. Massive tree planting in Africa will hinder desertification and global warming, which is one of the biggest threats in our world today. Trees will also be able to help poor farmers make more money, both short and long term. High-quality mahogany trees are in high demand with limited supply, so that is a proven way of good sustainable business.

Our *Vision* is:

> *To eradicate poverty and corruption in Africa*

Our *Mission* is:

> *By social entrepreneurship, plant as many trees as there are people on this planet, and thereby finance the sustainable implementation of the vision*

2. <u>Microfinance for Agriculture (non-profit)</u>

Most farmers in Africa survive on less than $2.00 a day. If we are ever going to eradicate poverty in Africa, we must help poor farmers make more money for themselves through entrepreneurial approaches, and microfinancing is a proven way to kick-start this process. This way, poor people borrow money to be able to start their own businesses, and thereby keep their dignity and build their self-confidence at the same time.

3. <u>Education of Children (non-profit)</u>

If children in Africa do not have access to free primary education, there is no way any African country will be able to eradicate poverty. The NGO "Child Africa" took on the job of building schools and educating children. My wife, Julie Solberg, has been the Managing Director since we started, and without her, there is no way we could have gotten the success we have experienced, as everyone can see that she works with a passion. We also know that poverty and corruption are closely related, so we teach children in the schools and universities the importance of being honest and having the integrity to fight corruption long term, through our "BINGWA" (Champion in Swahili) movement. We also teach the subjects of "Honesty and Integrity" in our three schools in Uganda. And we have BINGWA TV programs for the purpose of fighting corruption.

Another important thing people are not thinking about when it comes to sponsoring a child to go to school in Africa, is the fact that it is one of the best and most secure ways of "paying it forward" that exists. I had already experienced it many times since 1991 when my wife and I started Child Africa. You see, when children go through school and get an education, and when they later get married and have their own children, they will NEVER let their own children be illiterate, so they will find a way to educate them too. This way, saving ONE child means saving the whole coming generation after that child, and if that is not "paying it forward" and the best self-help ever, what is?

PAY IT FORWARD - IN DIFFERENT WAYS

The principle of "paying it forward" can be done in many different ways, from giving money directly to others and telling them to pay it forward, to just give them advice and ask them to pay forward the same or other advice to someone who needs it. OR, it can be built into a concept that benefits everyone involved, so it thereby becomes sustainable. Can you imagine a system where money is being paid forward to the three areas above? This is doing a lot of good by eradicating poverty and corruption in Africa over time, and at the same time, the ones who participate only in the money-making tree planting process, make money enough from that one profit-related process, and thereby automatically support the two others.

As you can imagine, all these areas of operation needed a good back office and database, as well as many websites, in order to follow up everything from partners to customers. I was lucky to get another partner with great integrity, Jan-Tore Øvrevik, a Norwegian data specialist, who has been the one responsible for most of our IT developments. Without him, it could not be done.

The little boy from the movie, "Pay It Forward," who came up with the idea of paying it forward and presented his idea in his school classroom, explained it this way:

"If I did good to three people and they all did the same to another three each, and these nine did the same to three more each, and if it continued forward, the world would be a much better place."

He was right, and IF they all did that, the world <u>would</u> probably be a much better place to live. However, it did not work out well for him in the movie, and it will probably not work out well for all others either, due to the fact that it depends on too many other people's goodwill, in order to succeed.

On the other side, not everybody HAD to succeed for the principle to be a success, because it would be a success for everyone it worked for, regardless of the levels it reached. My thinking that if there was a financial reward for anyone, it would make it more sustainable too, was right. THAT was actually what I found. With a financial reward for everyone, the success was assured, and people were continuing year after year with paying it forward.

After 13 years as a pilot project, more than 40,000 people mostly from the Scandinavian countries, but also from about 20 more countries around the world, have found out that, to "pay it forward" in a social entrepreneurship way, has already eradicated poverty for more than 10,000 partner farmers in Africa, and the number is increasing every day. Within the first 13 pilot years, one million trees were planted, but in the 14th year, another one million trees were planted in that year alone, and in the 15th year, another one million more trees were planted. And in the years ahead, we plan to double it every year until we reach our goal of planting one million trees each day in Africa.

We have also funded three microfinance banks, which are owned by the communities and which today are self-driven, which is helping over 5,000 families in a sustainable way. At the same time, three quality schools have been built in Uganda, and more than 20,000 children have been helped with education and been trained to fight corruption in several ways—through reading the free BINGWA magazine, singing and dancing the BINGWA song, participating in various school plays, and through BINGWA TV.

In April 2019, the BINGWA movement had 10,000 school children at the Kololo stadium in Kampala, Uganda, singing the "integrity song," and gave different performances, something that really touched all the dignitaries present and made its mark.

HEALTH AND WEALTH COMES TOGETHER

In 2020, the company, Better Globe Forestry Ltd, also started to plant the world's most medicinal tree called "Moringa" as another way of making money by doing good. It is also like paying it forward, as a self-help model, with the result of health AND wealth for the participants. The dried leaves of Moringa, made into powder and put in capsules, is probably the healthiest food supplement anyone can take for getting better health, as Moringa is said to ... "cure 300 diseases." The principle of paying it forward therefore works in two ways, because the people who tell someone about it make money by selling the product, as well as giving the new people better health by using it.

"Better Globe Forestry Ltd." will, in some years ahead, probably become the biggest tree planting company in the world, and they will make a huge difference for the environment, because they are transforming useless dryland into "greenland," which can be used to plant food and thereby fight poverty also. At the same time, they are mitigating global warming too. I believe that, when many people are coming together with the aim of doing good for underprivilege people, and as a bonus making money for themselves, nothing can be much better. That is the way I see it, the best way of paying anything forward. My experience is also that everyone who participates will never be the same again.

About Rino

Rino Solberg has been a consultant, speaker, coach, and serial entrepreneur for over 40 years. Since 2004, he is also Chairman/Founder of **Better Globe Group** and the non-profit, **Child Africa**. Born in Norway in 1944, he enrolled in the Norwegian Air Force in 1963 and took five years of engineering education. He dropped it in 1968, and his lifetime journey as an entrepreneur began. He started an electric appliance shop, which was the biggest in town when he sold it ten years later. He was then ready for more significant, and international challenges.

In 1976, Rino invented and got patents in 12 countries for a grinding machine – for valves that he called "Unislip" – and he had companies in Norway, the USA, Germany and Japan, and agents in 20 countries. He ran his companies successfully for 13 years, then he sold out and started a training company.

Rino is also an author who has written 12 books within the area of personal development/sales/business/leadership, and he has given over 1000 seminars in the above areas. As a consultant, he has trained over 150 companies to be certified to ISO 9000 / ISO 14001 series quality / environmental management standards, and he has been a motivational speaker and sales trainer for over 40 years.

In 1977 in Norway, he met his wife, Julie, who was born in Africa. In 1991, they started an NGO called Child Africa to help sponsor poor children through school. All these years of working in Africa, and seeing the poverty and struggle of the people there, got him to begin thinking about how he could use all the knowledge and skills he had acquired over the years to make life better for poor African people. (www.childafrica.org and www.bingwa.info)

In 2004, at 60 years of age, Rino decided to do something more valuable with the rest of his life than merely building businesses and working for money, and to find a goal that was much bigger than himself and something that could change the world. He elected to take on the biggest goal he could think of:

ERADICATE POVERTY AND CORRUPTION IN AFRICA

And he has been doing that with great success ever since – one family at a time.

You can connect with Rino at:
- rino@betterglobegroup.com
- www.betterglobegroup.com
- www.betterglobemedia.com
- www.betterglobeforestry.com

CHAPTER 3

THE FOUR ENGINES OF SELF-LEADERSHIP

HOW TO USE YOUR GIVEN POWER TO BREAK OUT OF YOUR POVERTY CHAINS?

BY DR. ALINE SIMEN-KAPEU

*Poverty is not an accident. It is man-made and can be removed
by the action of human beings.*
~ Nelson Mandela

Do you know that accepting your inability to expand your capacities and to have basic freedoms acts as a giant hurdle to your success? Nelson Mandela said: "Poverty is not an accident." During the past 25 years, I poured out my life fighting poverty. Spending time with poor people helps to understand that poverty has material, social, physical, intellectual, psychological, and spiritual dimensions. What are your bottlenecks to success? Are you in chains? Your mindset may be holding you back from the life you deserve. Your body may be stopping you from grasping opportunities. Your spirit may be blocking you from opening the gates of your reserved blessings. Your heart may be holding you from experiencing the richness of life. Take a moment to reflect.

Do you realize that you are surrounded by opportunities? If you cannot see them, it is most likely time to change the way you perceive your life and the world. This is YOUR CHOICE. Stop your life from leading you and lead your life. Achieving greatness requires careful attention to the body, mind, heart, and spirit, as the human condition is defined around these four domains. Stephen Covey talked about "the paradigm of the whole person" in his book, *The 8th Habit*. Your lockdown or poverty status can be physical, spiritual, emotional, and/or intellectual. In writing this chapter, my goal is to guide you on how to ignite the four engines of self-leadership while caring for your whole being, propel yourself to the next level while breaking out of your chains, and transform your life forever.

BE AWARE OF YOUR CHAINS

I grew up in high-stress environments in a country in Central Africa, constantly at high risk for learning, emotional, and behavioral deficits. At age 7, I was devastated by the divorce of my parents. My mother was a proud nurse fighting alone daily for the survival of her five children. At age 13, I was regularly in an emotional lockdown mode with a poor supportive social environment for a teenage girl. Three years later, my mother suffered from depression and high blood pressure and stopped working. We were in chains, overburdened by the financial, social, and emotional dimensions of poverty. My future was not looking bright to me. "How do I get out of this mess?" I said to myself.

In 1994, we received a surprise visit from Uncle Theodore around Easter, a well-known engineer and a family friend she had not seen for long. Our conversation was inspiring and refreshing. A surprised expression crossed his face when he learned that I was involuntarily taking a sabbatical year for critical reasons. He promptly offered to mentor me despite his busy schedule. I was mesmerized by his enlightened philosophy of life, his way of thinking, as he shared some life-shaking lessons on how to move from poverty to greatness. I wrote them down with excitement, but later, I did not invest myself to make them a reality in my personal life. My mother finally died at age 50. It was an emotional blow!

Three years later, I got married to Jean. I was proud of myself when I finally completed my medical degree. However, my excitement melted away when I faced reality: there were limited job opportunities for young doctors in a country going through a complex emergency with a high poverty rate. Going back to school was not an option, as the university was closed and online learning a privilege. Jean was unemployed. Our small family was financially squeezed, and it was an emotionally heavy burden to bear. I was just crying out to God for rescue.

IGNITE THE FOUR ENGINES OF SELF-LEADERSHIP

One day, I was lying on my bed in deep thoughts, and I suddenly remembered my conversation with Uncle Theodore. I rushed into my closet to look for my old journal. I opened my notes and read the four marching orders: Get up! Get through! Get smarter! Get deeper! God answered my prayers. These words, the four engines of self-leadership, struck me like a bolt of lightning. I immediately took the decision to change by really applying the lifesaving secrets of Uncle Theodore. I had to be committed and do more by boosting my whole life: mind, heart, body, and spirit. So, based on what I learned, this is how you can ignite the engines of self-leadership to break out of your chains:

A. Boost your body: Get up!

You must adopt the mindset that you cannot continue to stay paralyzed and lethargic. You must get up and take the initiative in order to climb over roadblocks. Michael Jordan said: "If you're trying to achieve, there will be roadblocks.

I've had them; everybody has had them. But obstacles don't have to stop you." Stand up now and move! Benefit from opportunities that new roads will certainly offer you when you face a roadblock:

- **Activate your eyes**. Look for the detour sign next to the roadblocks instead of sitting down and complaining. Start looking carefully beyond what you see as your actual situation. Can you see new resources, or an opportunity to start over or to develop a hidden talent?
- **Open your mouth and ears**. Be curious and ask questions. Find new pathways recently paved that you are not aware of. Listen to others: What are your current needs? What else can you do now? What skills can you gain now? 'Get out of your routine box.'
- **Dare to explore new pathways**. Don't hesitate to choose different or unpaved routes; they may be uncomfortable now but not tomorrow. Fear is always present but be bold and courageous. David Livingstone said: "If you have men who will only come if they know there is a good road, I don't want them. I want men who will come if there is no road at all."
- **Move your hands and feet**. Use your hands to intentionally respond to people's needs. Use your feet to visit your community and contribute to its development. The literature highlights the mental health benefits of being active, even by volunteering. People who give their time to others may also be rewarded with better physical health—including a lower risk of depression, lower blood pressure, and even a longer lifespan. Ensure also that you exercise regularly and eat a well-balanced nutritious diet.

B. Boost your heart: Get through it!

In the chapter of Proverbs of my favorite book, the wise man said: "Above all else, guard your heart, for everything you do flows from it." Galvanize your heart by guarding it against bearing the unnecessary burden of frustration, envy, lack of forgiveness, bitterness, and jealousy. This will give you inner strength and you will enjoy the absolute beauty of internal freedom. I urge you to choose to get through any state of emotional poverty:

- **Check yourself.** Are you aware of yourself: values, passions, aspirations, feelings, behaviors, strengths, and weaknesses? Have you ever sought honest feedback of your impact on others? Your emotions dictate your thoughts, intentions, and actions with superior authority to your rational mind. Develop a high level of emotional intelligence.
- **Get connected.** Do not only think of other people, but also connect with them. Success exists on multiple levels and is impossible without building relationships. Be intentional and step in without being asked. Start by thinking about what you can give and not what you can receive.
- **Offer grace time:** Free yourself from anger, destructive emotions, and lack of forgiveness. You must develop and maintain the capacity to forgive and accept yourself or others. Be the light in the dark room.
- **Get along with anyone.** Yes, it sounds hard and sometimes impossible. Try my advice and free a little space in your heart to make people feel important, or by showing them that you value their time, knowledge, and experience. Everybody deserves to be loved.

C. Boost your mental ability: Get smarter!

Knowledge will help you maximize your potential and unleash its fullness. Nelson Mandela was in prison, in lockdown status, but decided to prepare for the future by getting smarter. He deepened his learning in leadership and negotiation, and learned a new language to improve his communication. He read books and engaged prison leaders by soliciting their help to achieve his linguistic objectives.

He boosted his mental capacity and positively impacted the future of his nation. Knowledge will help you survive for longer than you should. Benjamin Franklin said: "An investment in knowledge always pays the best interest." He never finished school, but shaped his life through abundant reading and experience, and unflagging commitment to his country. To galvanize your mental ability:

- **Gain more knowledge.** You will not waste your time. This will enrich your capacity to think out of the box. Learning something new will drastically improve your achievements.
- **Choose to grow exponentially to change the course of your life.** Design your pathway of growth and take practical steps. Brian Tracy said: "Be a lifelong student. The more you learn, the more you earn."
- **Grasp your gold.** Develop your talents and lead the life that was freely given to you to fulfill your unique mission. Most people coming out of poverty confirmed that they used to sit in a comfortable chair without knowing that if they had also learned to climb on that same chair, they would have seen the golden bar they inherited in the locker above their head.

D. Boost your spirit: Get deeper!

Floodgates, also called stop gates, are adjustable gates used to control water flow in flood barriers, reservoirs, rivers, streams, or levee systems. Generally, the dam gates are opened only when the reservoir is unable to contain too much water. Pause one second. Is your spiritual life pouring out refreshing waters on you, and consequently on others, to such an extent that the gates must be opened? You may or may not be a person of faith like me, but the following actions are universal and will help you to move your life to the next level:

- **Guard the time to nourish your spirit daily.** I still remembered Uncle Theodore, staring at me and saying in his most serious voice: "Get deeper with God to force the opening of the floodgates and live to the fullest. Having a galvanized spirit connected to our Creator is the masterpiece of what I am sharing with you – my most important advice!"

- **Guard your vision – follow your calling.** Vision paints a picture of the calling at a specific time in the future. Discovering your personal vision helps you understand your talents and your comparative advantages. It helps you know how to create the greatest value for yourself, your family, your church, your community, and your work.
- **Move from dreams to actions.** Do not only think about your dreams; you should act on them by defining your specific goals and achievable milestones. As Martin Luther King, Jr. said: "You don't have to see the whole staircase, just take the first step."
- **Guard your values like a precious gift.** Do not compromise. Your values are the definition of your meaning. My mentor John C. Maxwell said: "When values, thoughts, feelings, and actions are in alignment, a person becomes focused and character is strengthened."

EXPERIENCE THE BREAKTHROUGH

Have you decided to free yourself? I was poor and resolved to change my paradigm, boost my self-leadership, and influence my future. I began by focusing on my vision of transforming the lives of poor people. I stopped blaming others, adopted a positive mindset, and started to serve my community as a volunteer. My first doors opened. I learned English as a second language in the United Kingdom and obtained a Ph.D. in Public Health in Finland. Another door opened. I became an International Civil Servant and made a difference in the lives of the most vulnerable populations. I am currently an International Mentor and Trainer who contributes to the birth of a new generation of servant leaders who will transform nations.

Whatever type of poverty you find yourself in while reading this chapter, believe that your exponential transformation can be a reality. Again, it is YOUR CHOICE. I learned that when life sucks you under from different angles, you can push the button of freedom, break the surface, and breathe again. You can choose to ignite the four engines of self-leadership and take the pathway of greatness.

YOU CAN DO IT!

About Aline

Dr. Aline Simen-Kapeu is a leadership expert, author, trainer and speaker. Aline is dedicated to helping individuals and groups in the areas of leadership development, professional skills, and personal growth. She is passionate about the development and transformation of youth and she is helping them to understand the value of their potential and personal growth, sharpen their leadership skills, and develop a larger pool of emerging leaders. Aline is currently serving as a mentor at the Canadian Society of International Health. Dr. Aline Simen-Kapeu has great experience and expertise in the training and development of individuals, communities, and organizations. Aline is an Executive Director with the John Maxwell Team, an internationally-recognized and certified Speaker, Coach and Trainer. She volunteers with Christian organizations to fulfill her God-given mission of transforming leaders into change agents.

Aline has a very informative, entertaining, engaging and motivating style to create incredible programs for her audiences. If you want to reach your full potential and become the person you were created to be, Aline is available to take your leadership and life to the next level. Aline offers you practical programs, applicable ideas, and concepts that will bring immediate changes and long-term results. Aline's training will enrich your attitude, rekindle your determination to succeed, and expand your self-confidence. You'll come away empowered, centered, and focused on your goals.

Dr. Aline Simen-Kapeu has traveled, worked, and provided her services to those in need in more than 30 countries on four continents, and speaks French and English. Dr. Aline Simen-Kapeu received her doctoral degree in medicine from the University of Bouake, Côte d'Ivoire, her Ph.D. in Public Health from the University of Tampere, Finland, and her diploma in social entrepreneurship from the University of Oxford, UK. She has studied, researched, written, and spoken for 20 years in the fields of medicine, global health, public health, social entrepreneurship, youth development, and community development.

Dr. Aline Simen-Kapeu is an International Expert and Global Health Advisor who served for many years at the United Nations. She was formerly a Researcher at the University of Alberta, Canada, and at the National Public

Health Institute in Oulu, Finland. She has received many awards and published more than 30 articles in her field of expertise. She has conducted high-level leadership missions and consulting assignments in global health policy development, strategic planning, and community development. Aline is happily married to Jean Kapeu, and they have three children.

CHAPTER 4

DRIVEN BY A NEW PURPOSE

BY DARYL L. KEMSLEY

*Knowing your life purpose is the first step toward living a truly
conscious life. A life purpose provides us with a clear goal,
a set finish line that you truly want to reach.*
~ Simon Foster

There is no better time to earn your success than right now. This sounds like a fulfilling life plan, right? At least it did to me. By the time I was twenty, I had started to earn the financial windfalls that my full-time entrepreneurship had rewarded me with. It was exciting—quite a thrill—and knowing I could never work another 9-5 made it even greater.

My work was in business startups. I was a finder for companies. What I found was big amounts of "success." It took a couple years of constant, vigorous work, and my ambition gladly took it all on.

It had already taken a lot of discipline and adapting true successful habits to reach what I believed to be success, leading to me being blessed with riches beyond what most people my age could achieve. Thirteen high-end cars bought and paid for. A big rent-free house with a driveway long enough for all my cars, plus some rent-free roommates with whom to spend time. Then there were the occasional trips and vacations around the world, fully embracing the high life and feeling invincible.

However, I was not invincible. So far from it. My lavish lifestyle of self-indulgence was not sustainable (thank goodness). Trying to operate life through the lens of ego had sold me on a future so many of us believe we want, but it has no connectivity to what guides your life from the inside out—the subconscious self.

It was only a surprise to me when things began to go wrong. I felt sabotaged, the result of a business partner whose mental illness became volatile and my naïveté that I could place all my eggs into one basket. My "success" was cut short—like a lifetime short. I was only 22 at the time. This was when I learned that both friendships and business can be "easy come, easy go." I was feeling used up and desperate to stick to something good in my life. What happened instead was a perpetuating sinking feeling.

As the months went by, things only grew worse. My BMW i8 was heavily vandalized by an old friend. My 1981 DeLorean, which was my childhood-rooted epitome of passion and the original reason for entrepreneurship, burnt down in a hit-and-run accident a few months later. It was not what happened to the vehicles that was as horrible as the price I paid for it. All this earned me a gruesome fifteen minutes of fame. My social media exploded, and people were cruel to me. At this point in my life, I had already replaced all my toxic relationships with local auto enthusiast communities to meet my social needs. People I would have gladly taken my shirt off my back for and considered my friends resorted to doxing and hazing, which led to even more vandalism and literal home-entering burglary attempts, until I could not even feel safe in the comfort of my now-empty home. There was so much injustice; my obsessive and untrained 22-year-old self could not take it any longer.

I slowly retreated from life, something not easy for an extrovert to do. It just felt safer to withdraw than to allow people in. For me, this meant:

1. My friends were gone, except for one. (Thank you, Zac.)
2. My business partner had submarined me and was gone.
3. My entire life's work vanished.

All that was happening became an excruciating and painful journey to endure. People are rarely supportive in person, projecting ignorance and knocking you down with unrelenting words. I took all this to heart, and it led to a pitiful stage in my life. Self-doubt crept in as I wondered if I was really such a disgrace like others seemed to think. For the next eighteen months, this was how I began to view myself.

I had enough left in savings to live comfortably for a while. But was I truly living? I was a suicidal guy who was usually in my basement, smoking weed and feeling bad about myself. I was mentally and emotionally drained and completely unmotivated to operate as anything else.

It took far too long for me to even consider rejecting the thoughts that had dominated my every day during this time. Then one day, something inside me shifted—only the slightest of shifts—and it allowed a glimmer of awareness into my mind. Now I thought, *it is not normal to want to change everything about myself.* What if my bitterness was misplaced all this time? Maybe it was not okay to hate yourself and feel like you were wasting oxygen in this world. What if God and life itself were providing me with exactly what I needed to escape the societal rat race entrepreneurs and innovators swear to live against?

By this time, my savings were down to my last $500. I had blown most of my money, not caring what I bought or why. Why would it matter when I might not be alive long enough to see it all spent?

Then something compelled me to try doing something, anything, to stop feeling like a hollow carcass. What I decided to do was the gateway to finally exploring my life's purpose.

HOME-LESS AND FINDING MORE

I got into my car and made the half-hour drive to downtown Salt Lake City. On the way, I stopped at McDonald's and purchased about $150 worth of food from their dollar menu. Not sure what to do next, I began to walk around. When I saw a homeless person, I asked them if they wanted some food, and this is what I did until all the food was given out.

This made me feel better. Finally, I gained a moment in time where I was a bit less lonely. Now don't get me wrong, there is nothing honorable about one lost guy handing out junk food to gain any sort of human connection. It was mostly an attempt to make me feel something I had not felt in a long while.

A profound moment then surfaced, in which I realized these homeless people were embracing me, literally. They would hug me and start to have a conversation with me. Who was helping who? It made me feel so good about myself. Maybe it was grace or the charitable act, but I felt a level of positivity that had eluded me for a long time. I used that positivity to spark a bit of the capitalist in me to ponder how to best continue what I had begun. Questions surfaced like:

- Next time I go to Salt Lake City, where am I going to go?
- Where are the most homeless people going to be?
- How am I going to plan my route?

Soon enough, my $500 was used up, and I was taking credit card advances out of the ATM to fund my feeding the homeless obsession. I did not pay my utilities and basic expenses, but I felt like this was the first thing that had ever truly made me happy. (It may have even been considered joy.) My band-aid solution had bought me peace, and it compelled me to think about how it was not a solid fix to any problem at all. It was a meal, nothing more, but it kept me going.

Slowly, I began to feel better. I was able to reflect on my own mental psyche and try to mend the lack of love I had for myself. I journeyed through my childhood, where I began in Hong Kong, the son of an Asian mother and American father. I delved into the qualities that were driven into me either consciously, or subconsciously as a child and accepted why they did not fit me as an adult. This liberated me. I recognized how I had been operating off scarcity. I had acted idiotically, an accumulative sum of a genuine soul operating through trauma and surviving through ego in a 'dis-genuine' society. I realized it was time to do a deep dive into the beliefs of my subconscious mind, and do the hard work of transforming them so I could serve myself better and thereby serve others better too.

Understanding how my past was a circumstance that did not have to be my future started forming. I grew to understand things had happened for me, not to me. This epiphany was the light at the end of the self-destructive life-long tunnel. And it was all I needed.

I spent the next months decluttering and preparing for my new life. I gave away most of my possessions—clothes, watches, cars, and made room for abundance into my life.

Now, when I received my random paychecks for royalties and such, I used them to pay down some debts. One check was used differently, though. It was roughly $2,500 and came from my YouTube channel, where I was a car journalist. This check was used to make an investment that cemented the importance of a *"pay it forward"* mindset. I started a non-profit, niceHuman. It was the start of a more permanent fix to just feeding the homeless in Salt Lake City.

The group I formed still fed the homeless, but we also engaged in conversations and talked to these people. They were societal misfits just like me and could get back on track as I had with some assistance.

It became easier for me to ditch my obsession with money for the sake of possessions, and not just because I was broke either. The money would return, and when it did, it would become my means to contribute something to others in whatever way I could, large or small. Also, I gave my time, which provided me with immense energy as I saw how this mattered as much, if not more than the donation. All this started my journey to renewed confidence and strength for life, and to reenter the business world with some new bits of wisdom, as a new man.

THREE STEPS FORWARD

I was privileged enough for life to give me an incredible do-over. This now helps me in many ways, including my business and my involvement in mankind's wellbeing. There are three lessons that stand out to me as fundamentally important for all people.

1. **Sacrifice helps you embrace what you deserve in life and business.**
   Sacrifice is necessary to break yourself down and build a life with a more solid perspective. This is not the type of sacrifice in which you give up everything for someone or something. I am referring to tough choices you make daily to begin recognizing your self-worth when it has been lost. It may require removing unhealthy relationships from your life, romantic or platonic, and a deep dive into your most inner thoughts, habits, and patterns. I did this, and it was not easy. It was, however, revealing and incredibly uplifting. My inspiration to make it through these times came from the little bit of joy I received while feeding the homeless. This offering from me to others catapulted the good emotions and feelings that helped me address some of my life's toughest moments.

2. The principles of building a business are consistent.

As the rebuilding of my career and life began, I learned I could use the same business principles to rebuild something new —and better. The better comes from the changes in the impact your results can have on others, not just your own personal wealth. This plays out daily: from the way my entire company helps clients start building up their own success to the endless reasons I am inspired to help others. The days where money was spent on luxury items and possessions to fill a personal void are through. Now the returns on my investments are designed to fuel the world to be a more inspired place, one act at a time. I have never felt more fulfilled than now.

3. When you listen for it, you will find the people that need you most.

Becoming alert to more than my immediate needs is something I find necessary to begin the joy of *"paying it forward"* in life. When I first experienced this, I could not have said what was taking place; it was a feeling more than just a conscious decision. The onset of positive energy that came when I offered something to those in need was my first clue about the greater picture.

- When friends wanted to find ways to become more financially stable, I was able to offer my services and direct them to the opportunities they could pursue.
- A friend I knew from the gym was homeless, and I hired him at my company. Then I proceeded to help him in the journey of realizing his worth so he could love himself, making it easier for him to become more for those he desires to help.
- Guiding those who wish to start small businesses receive a zero interest rate funding, as well as improve their credit scores to help them optimize their opportunities and lives.

All these ways of helping people are important. They are a

handful of the incredible journeys people take each day. Each one could be a chapter in a book on its own, but all represent how I have chosen to view my relationship with the rest of our human family.

A step forward for anyone has a ripple effect on those around them. Every action we choose to take to help another matters more than we often realize.

IT ALL BEGAN WITH A PURPOSE

Discovering your purpose is the most significant thing you will do in your life, and you, your loved ones, and the world will be better off because you went on this journey.
~ Mastin Kipp

My life journey began with chaos and a desire for more of all the wrong things. This disguised the void that was in my life. The more I tried to fill it, the emptier I became. Once life forced an end to it all, and after my emotional willingness to find love for myself began, everything started to evolve. Yes, I am still a work in progress—and I plan to be for my entire life.

Finding my purpose was the start of my healing. This purpose is greater than me and has allowed me to experience joy. This purpose is not to be happy all the time because this is not possible. However, finding joy is. Purpose and joy are good companions. With purpose, you are drawn to helping other people. It is not sustainable any other way. Today, I see how purpose gives all of us the breath of life needed to *"pay it forward"* and help others too. This is how I choose to live.

About Daryl

Business strategist, fintech entrepreneur, public speaker, social media personality, and CEO—these are the diverse roles of Daryl L. Kemsley. He started in the business world as his company's nation-wide, number one new sales rep. His next and last job as someone's employee was as a Mandarin-speaking customer service and sales rep, where he also earned the distinction as the number one rep in the company.

Daryl contributes his success to his innate ability to look at a business model and turn it upside down, increasing a company's revenue and profitability by many-fold. He has done this for several businesses, earning consulting fees and equity. Daryl is now co-founder and CEO of SelfStart, a fintech company that has automated the 0% interest funding process with machine learning technology.

SelfStart exists to help raise people to a better situation in life. This service also carries over into endeavors outside of SelfStart. Daryl is immensely passionate about helping children who are being grossly abused every day of their lives. He is compelled to contribute to the noble cause of Operation Underground Railroad, where he is currently working as the Executive Producer of their latest documentary, *It's Happening Right Here*.

To learn more about Daryl and SelfStart, please visit:
- SelfStart.io

To learn more about how you can help in the fight against human trafficking, please visit:
- www.ourrescue.org

CHAPTER 5

CREATE UNCOMMON MARKETING – BY BECOMING *MISSION DRIVEN*

BY NICK NANTON & JW DICKS

His aunt would bake cookies for him when he was a little boy. And the cookies were awesome. So awesome that he wanted to make them even…well, …awesomer. He always wanted things to be the best they could be and the cookies were no different.

But in the poor neighborhood where he was from, you didn't make it far on cookies. He had to find another way out. He dropped out of high school to join the Air Force. He eventually got his high school equivalency diploma, and, when he was done with his military service, he went to college to learn clerical skills. That, in turn, led to a big break – he got a job as a secretary at the William Morris Agency.

There, his winning personality allowed him to work his way up the ladder, until he became the agency's first African-American talent agent. He also found a great way to attract big clients; he would send them over a batch of his special cookies, made by himself with the killer recipe he developed when he was a boy.

The homemade treats brought him some sweet deals and suddenly, he found himself representing such huge music superstars of the time as *Simon & Garfunkel* and *Diana Ross & the Supremes.* And while that was hugely exciting for someone who came from such a humble background, he still couldn't shake the thought that his magical cookies were where his real fortune lay.

So he borrowed seed money from a couple of his multi-millionaire clients, *Marvin Gaye* and *Helen Reddy*, and opened his own store in Los Angeles. It was a success. Hollywood, however, was just one market. The trick was finding a way to market his cookies to the rest of the country.

Instead of hiring an advertising agency to create an expensive campaign that he couldn't afford, the would-be cookie entrepreneur turned to a friend he had recently met who worked at a P.R. firm. That friend, in turn, introduced him to the head of the Literacy Volunteers of America – and the three of them brainstormed a national P.R. tour where the entrepreneur wouldn't sell cookies. No, he would sell *literacy.* It was a cause he passionately believed in because he came from a neighborhood where many never learned how to read and write properly.

Suddenly, his winning personality was being displayed in *People Magazine, Time Magazine,* A&E's "Biography," NBC's "Today Show," ABC's "Good Morning America," *The New York Times, The Chicago Tribune,* plus thousands of daily and weekly newspapers, food trades, and local television stations all across America. Of course, his cookies, which were popping up on supermarket shelves all across America, were mentioned in all these media appearances.

And suddenly those cookies were selling like hotcakes.

Wally "Famous" Amos had become truly famous in one of the very first instances of modern "Cause Marketing" – still used to this day as a textbook example in universities of the power that *Mission Driven* marketing can generate above and beyond conventional selling. That power led Famous Amos to sell his brand and company to the Keebler corporation in 1998, when Famous Amos Cookies had reached an estimated value of $200 million.

It's been estimated by the Literacy Volunteers of America that Wally Amos brought the problem of illiteracy to the attention of more people than anyone else in history. He didn't just sell cookies – he did a lot of good in spreading an important message, or *paying it forward*.

Famous Amos is an excellent example of how being a *Mission Driven Company* can maximize your marketing potential. Now, when we say a company is Mission Driven, we mean it has a strong, positive high- profile purpose beyond just selling goods and/or services. In one way or another, it adds extra value to the standard business equation, or *pays it forward* in some way.

Believe it or not, having this kind of mission in place is becoming more and more of a *requirement for* a successful business in this day and age. Here are a few statistics that more than make that case, all taken from the 2013 Cone Communications Social Impact Study:

- 93% of all U.S. consumers say that when a company supports a cause, they have a more positive image (a number that continues to trend up – it was 85% in 2010).
- 91% of global consumers are likely to switch brands in order to support one associated with a good cause.
- 90% of Americans are more likely to trust and stay loyal to Mission Driven companies.
- 82% of consumers base buying decisions and what products and services they recommend on a company's support for a cause.

Is it any wonder, with numbers like that, Mission Driven marketing is gaining an increasing edge over the competition? Or that big business is noticing that edge?

According to a Forbes study in 2011:

- 93% of 311 global executives surveyed believed their company could, "create economic value by creating societal value."[1]
- 84% agreed that, "companies need to evolve their giving programs from simply giving money to broader social innovation."[2]

No less a business legend than Richard Branson acknowledges this *Mission Driven* trend by blogging about what he sees as *"a fundamental transformation taking place in our societies. This transformation is not a technological one – it might be enabled by technology, but it's driven by people and their changing attitudes to participation and change... Here at Virgin we've been using our social media channels to help mobilize support around issues like these... truly understanding what your business can do to make a difference is a critical starting point for any business that wants to thrive in the future. And to be open to how your business will need to change in this new world."*[3]

THE APPLE OF THE PUBLIC'S EYE

So far in this chapter, we've been dwelling a lot on the heavily-publicized "cause marketing" aspect of a mission – pro-social and frequently charitable endeavors with which businesses align themselves, as Famous Amos did, to create a halo effect around their operation.

But, your mission doesn't have to be limited to that category. It can simply be about the way you do business – and it can still connect with the public with the same power.

1. Forbes Insights, Management and Business Operations, Corporate Philanthropy The New Para- digm: Volunteerism. Competence. Results. http://www.forbes. com/forbesinsights/philanthropy_ csr_2011/#sthash.zKzMn9ws.
2. Ibid.
3. Branson, Richard. "Occupy Yourself." January 22, 2014, http://www.virgin. com/richard-branson/ occupy-yourself

Now, there have been millions of pages written over the years about the genius of Steve Jobs and Apple, but rarely within the context we're going to employ here: As an individual, he was completely *Mission Driven*. That Mission became an essential part of his personal brand and Apple's corporate brand when he was at the helm; it was the motivating factor behind all his products.

In 2011, when he introduced the iPad2, he made this statement: *"It is in Apple's DNA that technology alone is not enough - it's technology married with liberal arts, married with the humanities, that yields us the results that make our heart sing."* [4]

Now, can you imagine Bill Gates saying something like that? Or most CEOs for that matter?

Because Jobs himself stood for more than just technology, because he made Apple adhere to incredibly high goals for usability and style when it came to all of its products, he set a new standard for a *Mission Driven* business that he made sure extended to Apple's marketing.

Jobs constantly asked two questions when it came to the company's marketing:

Question #1: Who is Apple?

Question #2: What does Apple stand for and where do we fit in this world?

His answer to those questions – and, ultimately, Apple's mission:

"Apple believes that people with passion can change the world for the better. And those people that are crazy enough to think that they can, are the ones who actually do." [5]

4. Lehrer, Jonah. "Steve Jobs: "Technology Alone Is Not Enough", The New Yorker, October 7, 2011
5. Byerlee, Dana. "What Steve Jobs Knew About the Importance of Values to Your Company", Yahoo! Small Business Advisor, Tuesday, August 6. https://smallbusiness.yahoo.com/advisor/steve-jobs-knew-importance-values-company-235014359.html

Now, keep those words in mind, as we present some of the copy from one of the most famous Apple ad campaigns of all time, 1997's "Think Different":

"Here's to the crazy ones. The misfits. The rebels. The troublemakers. The round pegs in the square holes.

The ones who see things differently. They're not fond of rules. And they have no respect for the status quo. You can quote them, disagree with them, glorify or vilify them.

But the only thing you can't do is ignore them. Because they change things. They invent. They imagine. They heal. They explore. They create. They inspire. They push the human race forward.

We make tools for these kinds of people.

While some see them as the crazy ones, we see genius. Because the people who are crazy enough to think they can change the world, are the ones who do."

Few can do *Mission-Driven* like Steve Jobs did. And the pay-off for how well he marketed that Mission?

- Apple has won the CMO Survey Award for Marketing Excellence (chosen by the world's top marketers) for 6 years straight.
- Apple was voted the most Powerful Brand in the World in 2012 in a Forbes study.[6]

MASTERING *MISSION-DRIVEN* MARKETING

When you want to learn how to do something, you turn to the best for inspiration. In this case, Apple is undeniably the master – so let's close out this chapter with some "Apple Axioms" that

---

6. Koprowski, Evon. "Apple Is the Most Powerful Brand in the World, According to New Forbes Study", Storyism.net, October 12, 2012. http://storyism.net/apple-is-the-most-powerful-brand-in-the-world-according-to-new-forbes-study

illustrate the most important *Mission-Driven* marketing lessons we've learned from this icon for the ages.

Apple Axiom #1: STAND FOR SOMETHING OR STAND FOR NOTHING.

If you check out the online website, UrbanDictionary.com, you'll find one of the terms listed is "Apple Hater," whose definition reads in part, "Apple haters dislike the success of the company and attempt to undermine consumers." Yes, because Apple's success has created a furtive and specially huge band of followers, there had to be a backlash. Whenever a company like Apple, a company with a firm, fixed identity and, yes, mission, stands out from the herd, there will be those who hate it just so they can also stand out from the herd.

As long as your mission has the right combination of attributes, you shouldn't concern yourself if your marketing happens to alienate a small portion of your potential customer or client base. It's inevitable – and it also makes your mission seem that much more authentic in the eyes of the public. You're not afraid to lose a few customers that don't believe in your mission. As long as you're positive and pro-active, never defensive and angry, small pockets of protest won't make the smallest dent in your brand.

Apple Axiom #2: YOUR PEOPLE MUST REPRESENT YOUR MISSION.

If you've ever been to an Apple Store, you know that the personnel is selling the Apple company culture just as much as its individual products. That's because Apple is careful to make sure their employees fully *understand and represent their mission.* In the words of one, "Sometimes the company can feel like a cult. Like, they give us all this little paper pamphlet, and it says things like—and I'm paraphrasing here—'Apple is our soul, our people are our soul.' Or 'We aim to provide technological greatness.'" [7]

---

7. Anonymous, "Confessions of an Apple Store Employee", Popular Mechanics, December 21, 2012

Your marketing isn't just about selling your mission to your potential customers, it's also about selling your mission to your employees and representatives – even, in some cases, your vendors. Zappos is another company that takes this principle very seriously, being so careful to make sure their employees fully support their company culture that, in the past, they've offered them money to quit!

Apple Axiom #3: KEEP THINGS SIMPLE.

Is there anything simpler – or more iconic – than the Apple logo itself? And is there anything more brilliant than including a sticker of that logo in every iPhone box?

Apple's actual mission is a fairly complex one – and yet the company is brilliant at communicating its essential essence with incredibly basic messaging. How basic? How about introducing such seminal products as the original Macintosh computer, the iMac and the iPod with just one word – "Hello."

Okay, they got a little wordier with the iPhone – those ads used the tagline, "Say hello to iPhone."

You might ask, well, what does saying "Hello" actually have to do with Apple's Mission? Plenty. Each new Apple product has a certain distinct "cool" look that immediately reflects the company's mandate to continually create beautiful new gadgets that deliver as much cutting- edge style as technology. Simply showing one of their new products with a friendly greeting says to the average consumer, "We did it again!"

Or, in other words, Mission Accomplished.

Apple Axiom #4: INFLUENCE THE INFLUENCERS.

In order to introduce the first Macintosh personal computer, Apple aired a special commercial nationally *only one time* – during the 1984 Super Bowl. And this was no quickie; it was directed by a major movie director, Ridley Scott (*"Alien,"* *"Blade Runner," "Gladiator,"* etc.) at the then-unheard-of price of $900,000. "1984," which was the title of the ad, ended up in the Clio Hall of Fame and was named to *Advertising Age's* 50 greatest commercials of all time.

But before all that happened, just after the commercial was completed and before it aired, it was screened for the Apple Board of Directors. They *hated* it. As a matter of fact, they never wanted it to see the light of day. Jobs insisted, the spot ran for its single airing during the Super Bowl, and the rest is history.

The commercial was more than an advertisement for the Macintosh itself – it was designed to create a conversation about the transformation of society through PCs. As Brent Thomas, the art director of "1984" said at the time, Apple "had wanted something to stop America in its tracks, to make people think about computers, to make them think about Macintosh...This was strictly a marketing position." [8]

Apple's marketing has always been as much about reaching the intelligentsia as its customer base. By aiming at influencing the influencers, their marketing achieves a high degree of credibility and prestige that goes beyond the usual retail selling. "1984" made everybody talk about Apple, even though the ad itself disappeared forever (well, you can still watch it on YouTube). Its "once-and-done" nature just made it all the more compelling.

You also want your organization's mission to be understood and respected by those in a position to validate and amplify your marketing message. Third party validation is always an incredible positive for any marketing campaign. The more "buzz" you can create for your mission, the more you impact the general culture.

---

8. Burnham, David. "The Computer, the Consumer and Privacy." The New York Times, March 4, 1984

Apple Axiom #5: AVOID CONFLICT BETWEEN YOUR MARKETING AND YOUR MISSION.

Anyone who studies marketing remembers the "1984" commercial. But very few talk about its follow-up.

In 1985, Apple presented another "event" commercial for the Super Bowl, designed to capitalize on the massive impact they had made the year before. Apple actually placed full page ads in newspapers around the country, telling readers to make sure and watch during the third quarter for their new sensational commercial – and gave special cushy seats and signs to everybody in the stadium at the actual Super Bowl.

All of this ballyhoo resulted in one of the company's biggest marketing failures. This commercial was received so poorly, Apple didn't place another ad in the Super Bowl for another 14 years!

The ad was called "Lemmings", and its purpose was to introduce Apple's new Macintosh Office software. It did this by portraying hundreds of blindfolded businessmen and women walking off a cliff to their doom – insinuating that everybody using a PC instead of a Mac was, basically, a self-destructive sheep. Problem was, many more people fit into the former category rather than the latter. As one journalist put it, "Turns out that insulting the very people you are trying to sell merchandise to is not the best idea." [9]

"1984" dramatized someone changing the status quo in an exciting and vivid way; "Lemmings" dramatized hordes of people willingly walking into an abyss to die. One vision was stimulating – the other was just plain depressing.

Apple's mission, up until then, had been to inspire new ways of

---

9. Seibold, Chris. "January 20, 1985: Apple Goes to the Well One Too Many Times." AppleMatters.com, January 20, 2011. http://www.applematters.com/article/january-20-1985-apple-goes-to-the-well-one-too-many-times/

thinking and doing – "Lemmings", in contrast, was more of a scare tactic to motivate people into buying Apple products. It was a rare misstep by THE master marketer – and it demonstrated the necessity of keeping the spirit of whatever your Mission might be in whatever marketing you're currently planning.

The melding of mission and marketing is an incredible plus for any entrepreneur, business or nonprofit organization. It reinforces all the benefits that your Mission brings to the table, while elevating your marketing above the crowd with a subtext that stands out. And that, in turn, makes you Uncommon among your competition.

About Nick

An Emmy Award-Winning Director and Producer, Nick Nanton, Esq., produces media and branded content for top thought leaders and media personalities around the world.

Recognized as a leading expert on branding and storytelling, Nick has authored more than two dozen Best-Selling books (including *The Wall Street Journal* Best-Seller, *StorySelling™*) and produced and directed more than 50 documentaries, earning 16 Emmy Awards and 36 nominations. Nick speaks to audiences internationally on the topics of branding, entertainment, media, business and storytelling at major universities and events.

As the CEO of DNA Media, Nick oversees a portfolio of companies including: The Dicks + Nanton Agency (an international agency with more than 3,000 clients in 63 countries), Dicks + Nanton Productions, Ambitious.com and DNA Films. Nick is an award-winning director, producer and songwriter who has worked on everything from large scale events to television shows with the likes of Steve Forbes, Ivanka Trump, Sir Richard Branson, Larry King, Jack Nicklaus, Rudy Ruettiger (inspiration for the Hollywood Blockbuster, *RUDY*), Brian Tracy, Jack Canfield (*The Secret*, creator of the *Chicken Soup for the Soul®* Series), and many more.

Nick has been seen in *USA Today, The Wall Street Journal, Newsweek, BusinessWeek, Inc. Magazine, The New York Times, Entrepreneur® Magazine, Forbes* and *Fast Company*, and has appeared on ABC, NBC, CBS, and FOX television affiliates across the country, as well as on CNN, FOX News, CNBC, and MSNBC coast-to-coast.

Nick is a member of the Florida Bar, a member of The National Academy of Television Arts & Sciences (Home to the EMMYs), co-founder of The National Academy of Best-Selling Authors®, and serves on the Innovation Board of the XPRIZE Foundation, a non-profit organization dedicated to bringing about "radical breakthroughs for the benefit of humanity" through incentivized competition and best known for its Ansari XPRIZE—which incentivized the first private space flight and was the catalyst for Richard Branson's Virgin Galactic. Nick was a recipient of the Global Shield Humanitarian Award in Feb. 2019.

Nick also enjoys serving as an Elder at Orangewood Church, working with Young Life, Entrepreneurs International and rooting for the Florida Gators with his wife Kristina and their three children, Brock, Bowen and Addison.

Learn more at:
- www.NickNanton.com
- www.CelebrityBrandingAgency.com
- www.DNAmedia.com

About JW

JW Dicks, Esq., is the CEO of DN Agency, an Inc. 5000 Multimedia Company that represents over 3,000 clients in 63 countries.

He is a *Wall Street Journal* Best-Selling Author® who has authored or co-authored over 47 books, a 7-time Emmy® Award-winning Executive Producer and a Broadway Show Producer.

JW is an Ansari XPRIZE Innovation Board member, Chairman of the Board of the National Retirement Council™, Chairman of the Board of the National Academy of Best-Selling Authors®, Board Member of the National Association of Experts, Writers and Speakers®, and a Board Member of the International Academy of Film Makers®.

He has been quoted on business and financial topics in national media such as *USA Today, The Wall Street Journal, Newsweek, Forbes, CNBC.com,* and *Fortune Magazine Small Business.*

JW has co-authored books with legends like Jack Canfield, Brian Tracy, Tom Hopkins, Dr. Nido Qubein, Steve Forbes, Richard Branson, Michael Gerber, Dr. Ivan Misner, and Dan Kennedy.

JW has appeared and interviewed on business television shows airing on ABC, NBC, CBS, and FOX affiliates around the country and co-produces and syndicates a line of franchised business television shows such as *Success Today, Wall Street Today, Hollywood Live,* and *Profiles of Success.*

JW and his wife of 47 years, Linda, have two daughters, and four granddaughters. He is a sixth-generation Floridian and splits his time between his home in Orlando and his beach house on Florida's west coast.

CHAPTER 6

HOW TO GROW A SUCCESSFUL REAL ESTATE TEAM

BY SHELLY SALAS

Once you've made the decision that this is your next career move, how do you take off? What do you do first? What do you do second or third? You get my drift. These are all questions you must answer if your goal is to build a successful real estate team. In this chapter, you will learn about my failures and successes, and hopefully, I can help you skip some of the overwhelming headaches I faced along the way.

Depending on whom you ask, success is defined in many different ways. To some people, success is defined by having a spouse for many years, children, being healthy, having money, the career you've always wanted, or having freedom in your life. There is definitely no wrong way (I think) of defining success. We all have our own version of what success looks like. For me, it's a combination of all these items. I am one of the lucky ones who was fortunate enough to meet an amazing man over 20 years ago (my babe Luis) and who still, to this day, is my biggest cheerleader. I was blessed to have three amazing children with my hubby, and I'm fairly healthy, I love my career, and I am able to get more freedom as time goes on. I feel pretty blessed in life, and I'm at that phase where I want to help as many people truly enjoy their career as I do.

It wasn't always this way, of course. In the beginning, my husband and I were the only two in our company. We would work long hours, and sometimes it felt like we were working 20-hour days. At that time, we were full-time college students with children, working real estate, and at one point, we had a car dealership as well in the middle of all this (just because we had "extra time"). As I reflect on this now, it brings a smile to my face as I nod side to side. How did we do this? When did we sleep? Oh, the beautiful memories we made together and as a family. I wouldn't trade that for the world; well, maybe for more sleep.

That's how we started, but now I am the team leader of the number one team in our area. We help more families get into or out of a home than any other real estate team hands down! We're focused on client experience. We want to make sure that every client that walks in through our doors leaves with the best possible experience they can get while buying or selling a home. To us, it doesn't matter whether you are buying a $5,000.00 piece of land or that million-dollar home. Our *2nd mile service* is reserved for all of our clients, no matter the price range.

Why are we so focused on experience? Well, …quick side story. I remember when my husband and I went to a high-end dealership. At that time, we were in a rental because I was involved in an accident and had a "loner" vehicle. I only had the "loner" for a few days, so we were on a bit of a time crunch. We did the research, I knew what vehicle I wanted, so as long as it drove fine and everything worked, I was leaving with that vehicle that day. My husband and I walked into the dealership (full disclosure, we were in sweatpants, t-shirt, and tennis shoes) we were standing in the lobby, and we were completely ignored. Not only did they make us feel like we did not belong there, but they looked at us like we could not afford to buy a vehicle at their dealership. It is one of the worst feelings. Anyways, they finally called someone from the back to "assist" us. We bought the car and came to pick it up the next day. When we walked into the dealership this time (in full disclosure again, we were in our business attire), the number of salespeople that wanted to assist us this time was crazy. Ever since then, we have made it our duty; it is our philosophy that everyone gets the *2nd mile service* treatment no matter what they are buying.

We are going to start off by reverse engineering your team. What do I mean by this? I am going to help you take your goal (whatever that is) and just work our way backward. The first thing you must do is get into your workspace and make sure you are in "the zone." We all have our own version of what that is; I would share mine with you, but then that would be another side story, and I know you want me to get you to the finish line quickly. Perhaps in my next book, I will talk about my "zone" more.

Now that you are in your zone and you are ready to start, write down what your goal is. Are you creating your team based on the number of families you want to help, the amount of Gross Commission Income (GCI) you want to make, the total number of agents you would like to have, or by total sales volume? Again, no wrong answer here, you just have to put it in writing.

> *A dream written down with a date becomes a goal.*
> *A goal broken down into steps becomes a plan.*
> *A plan backed by action makes your dreams come true.*
> ~ Greg S. Reid.

Writing my goals down on paper was something my husband taught me to do, and it was one of the best tips I could have ever received. So, I'm sharing this with you as well.

Now that your goal is written down, the next step is for you to calculate some numbers. Let's say you are growing your team based on a certain gross commission income (GCI) that you want to make. Great. What is the average sales price in your office or market? I say this because sometimes they are not always the same. If you only work higher-end deals, then obviously, your average sales price will be higher, compared to the market average since you are not selling $50,000.00 homes, etc. So now you have established your average sales price, how many deals do you need to close in order to reach your desired gross commission income (GCI).

Now that you know how many deals you need to meet your goal of "x", you know how many people you will need around you to accomplish this. For this chapter's purpose, let us say you need 100 closed transactions to get to your gross commission income (GCI) goal. How will you close 100 families? You know your market, what does a "go-getter" agent's production look like? Let's say that you are that "go-getter" and you're currently helping 50 families a year. That's awesome! That's a lot of families, but let's face it, not everyone is as driven as you are, so the other agents are probably closing about 25 deals a year or less. Just to be clear, 25 deals are nothing to frown upon, especially since, according to the National Association of Realtors, the average real estate agent sells about 12 homes a year. However, your goal is 100 families per year. If you help 50 families, we will need at least four additional agents to help you with the other 50 families. I am using the NAR statistics of 12 closings per year to cover the other 50 needed families. One of these agents should be able to handle 14.

Based on these figures, you will need a team of five selling agents (you "the-go getter," and four additional agents) to handle 100 families. Yay! Your team is slowly growing. You're building your business plan. This is what a rainmaker does. The next step is to focus on your support team. If you have a team of five that are aggressively selling, you will need admin support for the day-to-day activities. When I have my team of five, I had three support team members. They had various roles, but it all flowed well because of the systems and processes I had in place. You must take the time to analyze what is "admin" work for your office. Each team defines these roles differently. I have visited some teams that I feel are severely overstaffed for their production numbers, but it works for them.

That brings me to what I feel is one of the most crucial things that will allow you to become not only successful but efficient at the same time. Systems and processes! Yes, this is super important! You may be able to get away with not having systems and processes in place when you are a solo agent because you know what to do each step of the way. But when it is no longer just you, you need everyone to handle every client the same way you do—every single time. Referrals will come to you over and over if your entire team is giving all your clients the "wow" service each time. Putting together systems and processes will save you so many headaches (trust me). And what you will find is that as you continue to grow, you will have to tweak your process a tad bit along the way to accommodate your growth changes.

My advice to you is to secretly shop your processes and systems at least once a year to ensure that everything is flowing the way you think it is flowing. I say the way that "you think it is flowing" because what I learned throughout the years is that if there is a way to do a short cut, it will be done. So, every single step must be in a plan or task, or it will not be done. That fabulous employee you have right now that completes a step for you that is not written down but "knows to do it because someone told them" won't be there forever, and when they leave, that step now has fallen through the cracks, but you may not be aware. This was a lesson I learned as I grew along the way. Heck, I'm in the process of updating my systems now. I know it's crazy, but I like to look over our systems and processes a lot to see if there is a more efficient way of doing things, or if there is something that will benefit our clients more.

Let us recap, you wrote down what your goal is, you calculated how many salespeople you will need to achieve your goal. We discussed that you will now need to figure out how much admin support you will need in order to fulfill your goal. And we covered the importance of having systems and processes in place in order to make everything flow smoothly. I also mentioned that it is vital that you secretly shop your team at least once a year to make sure the process is flowing the way that you would like for it to flow.

This is it! You now have a quick guide on how to create a successful real estate team. It is this simple. I know that if I was able to do it, so can you! Put your goals in writing and hang them on your wall where you can see them daily. This will not only help you stay focused on your end goal, but it will serve as a daily reminder on what to focus on and prioritize daily. It is very easy to focus on other non-rainmaker activities or get pulled into "got-a-minute" meetings, so this will always bring your focus back.

I am so passionate about what I do. I love it! I don't see this as work; it's just my life, my fun life.

About Shelly

Shelly Salas is the Team Leader of the number one team in Central Texas. She went from being a solo agent alongside her husband working only with bank-owned properties, to helping thousands of families get into or out of a home. She has been ranked number one in Texas and number two in the entire nation by NAHREP for the past several years. She has consistently ranked in the top 1% in the Nation as advertised in *The Wall Street Journal* Real Trends ranking report, and Americas Best Real Estate Professionals.

As an Army Veteran, Shelly is able to apply the leadership skills she gained while in service to train her team, and she also applies her knowledge gained from her Psychology degree when mentoring her team and analyzing and solving a problem.

Not only does Shelly help clients buy and sell real estate, but she is also an investor herself. She has flipped many homes throughout her career. She is still actively buying and selling real estate for her own real estate portfolio. She uses her experience and knowledge of investing and shares this knowledge with her team and investor clients. She says: "You can find us on Facebook to see what my team looks like: facebook/thesalasteamrealtors."

Shelly also co-authored another Best-Selling Book called *Real Estate Game Changers* and is the host of the Shelly Salas Real Estate Show. The radio show streams live every Sunday alongside her co-host and dear friend, Melissa Reyes.

Shelly owes her work ethic to her upbringing. Working since she was a child in the orange, cucumber, and watermelon fields from sunup to sundown, she definitely never shy's away from working long hours when needed. Her joy in life is helping other people reach their heart's desire, whether it is a team member or a client.

She loves to give back. Every year, together with her team, she donates thousands to the Children's Miracle Network, and together they also give individually-wrapped Christmas gifts to hundreds of children in low-income areas each year.

Shelly has been married for over 20 years to her husband, Luis, and together they have three wonderful children, Bryonna, Louis, and Michael. Real Estate is her passion, but her family is her life.

You can connect with Shelly at:
- shelly@thesalasteam.com
- www.facebook.com/thesalasteamrealtors
- www.shellysalas.com

CHAPTER 7

THE "SMALL" FAVOR

BY STEVEN ALVEY

I've always found it incredible how the smallest, seemingly insignificant decisions can lead to colossal effects later on. Domino Effect, Butterfly Effect, whatever you call it, it's a fascinating phenomenon.

Of course, that phenomenon can be either good or bad. A single musket shot in Lexington leads to the revolutionary war. ...Percy Spencer keeping a chocolate bar within a few inches of a radar device, gives us the microwave. ...Hitler's aide absentmindedly scooting Von Stauffenberg's briefcase bomb just a few inches to the left—you get the idea.

But I'd like to focus on the "good" side of this phenomenon. Specifically, in keeping with the "pay it forward" theme of this book, I want to draw particular attention to the idea that acts of gratuitous kindness tend to reap positive rewards for those who do them. It's a phenomenon that my father related to me many years ago, after having experienced it many times in his life. If you focus, in life or business, on providing positive value and service to others, especially when you don't ask for anything in return, it can pay dividends for you later on.

In this chapter, I'd like to share a story of how a random (and frankly, very small) act of kindness that I did for a fellow entrepreneur four years ago quickly snowballed into a massive amount of totally unexpected business success (and possibly ensured the very existence of my business today).

But, before we get to all of that, allow me to set the sad, unfortunate scene in which this small act of kindness took place. It was April of 2016, and I was sitting upstairs in the spare bedroom-turned-home-office of our duplex in Bellevue, Nebraska. I had just left a more than decade-long Air Force career and determined that I was going to "start an online business" no matter what it took. Everyone thought I was crazy. Why not stay in another nine years and get that fat lifelong pension? And sitting in that room in front of the computer, there were parts of me wondering if they were right. I was wondering if I'd made a big mistake.

It wasn't that the startup itself (a cool, lead-gen software) was likely to fail. It was the timing. For various reasons, it was going to be about six months before I could fully "launch" the business publicly. The problem was... how was I supposed to provide for my wife and four kids (fifth kid on the way at the time – seven now) during that interim period?

I had no significant income, except for the $400 or so from the Air Force Reserves (I had decided to do the one weekend-per-month thing for a couple of years before going 100% civilian). Our small savings, consisting mostly of a recent tax refund and my final Air Force paycheck, were dwindling. Van payments, a hefty rent (which until a month prior had been covered by the Air Force), bills, groceries, and more, were quickly eating away at our small stash. On top of that, my four-year-old son had just suffered a kidney failure which, thanks be to God, had been caught just in time and resolved, but was going to require a whole lot of expensive treatment and added another layer of worry and uncertainty to the mix.

Somehow, I was going to need to get the family through that

chaotic moment and financially bridge that gap between then and the public launch of my startup six months later. But how? I was running out of ideas. I was even starting to look into the possibility of entering Nebraska's welfare program and looking for a local job. Something I wanted to avoid at all costs, as I knew that if I started down that "employee route," I'd be likely to get pulled fully in that direction and give up on the entrepreneurial dream. No, ...better to burn the ships.

So, there I was ... sitting in front of the computer ... anxious, depressed, and feeling like a total failure, when suddenly, it happened.

A SMALL FAVOR FOR A FELLOW STUDENT

I had recently joined a startup coaching program that I was using to help launch my business. It was an excellent program, run by a guy named John Thornhill in the UK, and I was, at that moment, interacting with some fellow students in their private Facebook group. One of those fellow students, a lady named Galina, had just launched her own first product through the program and was posting her initial results in the group. She mentioned she was having some payment processor problems, and her sales weren't great.

It was a pretty cool product. Basically, a training program that helped budding internet entrepreneurs research and choose a niche and a target market. The sales page wasn't half-bad, but, being a video guy, the first thing I noticed was that she had no sales video at the top (a huge factor in determining your conversion rates).

As I reflected on the absence of this crucial missing piece, the craziest idea popped into my head. What if I just made one for her? I had some pretty solid experience making basic animated videos. I had done it as a not-so-profitable side-gig for a few years prior on a micro-job site called Fiverr. I scrolled up and down her page to see what I had to work with, text and graphics-wise, and I quickly calculated in my head approximately how long it would take for me to crank out a concise video that summed up her offer. Maybe an hour or so.

I asked her in the group if she'd like me to produce one, and she quickly answered, "That'd be great! What would you need from me?" The answer was "nothing," but I didn't bother replying – I was already on the job. I went down the page, right-clicking and saving all the main graphics and images to my computer. Then, I opened a Word document and looked at her sales copywriting. I got a feel for the headlines, the bullet points, the overall selling proposition and so on, and immediately started typing up a short 90-second script that got the persuasive sales message across and ended with the slightly cliché, but always reliable "then click the button below and let's get started" call-to-action.

I recorded the voice over and proceeded to create a mostly text-based video in my animation software, added the graphics from her sales page, threw in an animated lady who popped on screen periodically emitting various emotional gestures in sync with the script, slapped on a catchy background music track and BOOM— we had a solid, not-too-shabby sales video. It took all of about an hour and a half.

I posted it in the group, along with instructions on how to download and embed it.

And that's when it began. …*The Domino Effect!*

Everything about my predicament changed in the moments that followed, although most of it was happening behind the scenes on the other side of the Atlantic, and I wouldn't find out about it all until a few days later.

Immediately, there was a huge buzz in the group. Not only was Galina ecstatic and very gracious about the small favor, but some members of the program's staff had noticed as well. One of the staff, a guy in Yorkshire by the name of Simon, clearly appreciated the fact that I had just done a service that many freelancers would have charged at least $500 to $1,000 for, in around 90 minutes, totally for free, for a fellow student. But even beyond that, what he and another of the staff had also noticed was my sales abilities, the way in which I had been able to weave together a coherent, persuasive pitch based on the main selling points on her product page. In one of his comments, he hinted at what was going on off-screen: "I sense a disturbance in the force, which could mean a lot of work is coming your way."

The Domino Effect that had begun behind the scenes apparently went something like this. Simon had been the first to notice and sit through the video. He immediately grabbed the phone and called his business partner, Randy Smith, also in Yorkshire. Randy picked up and said, "Hang on a minute, mate, I'm just watching a video that's been posted in the group." Of course, it was my video. They discussed it and contacted the big man, John himself, who, if I recall, was down the road "having a pint" and was intrigued by the development. They all agreed that it was an impressive video, cranked out in an impressively short amount of time. But there was another idea on their minds.

The thing was, Randy and Simon, in addition to being staff-members for John's program, were also "contractors" for a big international multi-million dollar company. One of the oldest, most trusted outfits in the internet marketing space, run by a couple of guys named Simon Hodgkinson and Jeremy Gislason. And they happened to be in need of... a video guy.

This entire narrative of events was relayed to me by Randy during a Skype call a few days later, (in arguably the thickest northern English accent the world has ever heard – I had watched enough old BBC series to make out a word or two here and there) at the end of which, he asked me if I'd be interested in doing some contract work for this company. The introduction happened. I was given a "trial job" by Jeremy a couple of days later, and within about a week had agreed to contracts for thousands of dollars' worth of work in the coming couple months and, unofficially, tens of thousands more through the end of the year.

God is good. Just like that, within about a week, I had gone from completely hopeless and wondering how on earth I'd feed my family, to having our financial future, at least for that interim period until my launch, totally secure. All because of one little 90-minute act of kindness.

And the jobs didn't end there. Even after my startup launched successfully, it was still a rocky road in the early days, and the jobs from Simon and Jeremy on the side just kept coming, eventually adding up to over $60,000 in contracts. Granted, $60K doesn't sound like a lot, especially looking back at it now, but it was a game-changer at the time.

But even that wasn't all. Because I was now "on their team" so to speak, I was able to seek this incredible company's support on future product launches of my own. They kindly agreed and came on board as sales affiliates, sending vast amounts of buyer traffic into my sales funnels over the years. You have to understand; these guys were behemoths in the industry. Everyone coveted them. Some of the most famous names regularly tried and failed to get them on board as affiliates, but they supported an insignificant newcomer like me.

All-told, after four years of contract work, affiliate partnerships, and joint venture partnerships with these guys, this relationship has produced hundreds of thousands of dollars in revenue for both our businesses. And that isn't counting the indirect and "uncountable" impacts, such as how many other sales affiliates have sent us traffic because they saw Simon and Jeremy's involvement with us or the immeasurable sales knowledge I gained from working with these two titans.

All thanks to one little act of kindness for someone else, with nothing expected in return.

So, how do you leverage this phenomenon in your life or your business? The opportunities are likely all around you. You just need to know where to look.

It might be that potential coaching client who you spend an hour with on the phone, free of charge, genuinely trying to help them solve a problem. It might be the quick but effective website you build for a non-profit or a struggling mom-and-pop store to help them bring in more customers. It might be a local church or charity where you volunteer your expertise or services, pro bono. Any of these small things could reward you later on down the road, either with more business, or a glowing testimonial that goes viral on social media, or positive PR of some kind.

But, ideally, you shouldn't attempt to find or manufacture these situations in a mechanical or calculated way. Just keep your eyes open for opportunities. Run your business or your career in a way that focuses on serving others and delivering value, and you'll reap the rewards in time.

About Steven

Steven Alvey helps people "sell more and sell better." He is an internationally-recognized sales and marketing expert who specializes in conversion maximization and customer value maximization (a fancy word for getting each customer to spend more money with your business).

Additionally, as an Executive Director of the John Maxwell Team, Steven also helps executives and teams implement high-level leadership, management, and communication practices in their organizations.

He has spoken on stages across the country, trained and empowered countless entrepreneurs all around the world, and has been featured on the cover of *Home Business Magazine*.

He has been endorsed and praised by famous entrepreneurs like Brian Tracy, who said, "it's absolutely crucial you work with Steven Alvey right now," Shark Tank's Kevin Harrington, who said, "Steven knows a thing or two about beating the odds," and Entrepreneur on Fire host, John Lee Dumas, who says, "give him a holla and you'll be prepared to ignite."

When he's not improving businesses and empowering entrepreneurs, Steven enjoys raising chickens and growing tomatoes on his acreage in the Midwest, where he lives with his wife Emily and their seven children. Yes… seven.

You can connect with him at:
- Steven@StevenAlvey.com
- www.Facebook.com/Steven.warlord

CHAPTER 8

EMPOWER YOURSELF AND BE A PROFESSIONAL LEARNER

BY DAISY SHUK YIN NG

The LinkedIn "2020 Workplace Learning Report" reflects a global training trend that 51% of learning and development (L&D) professionals plan to launch upskilling training programs, while 43% plan to launch re-skilling programs to their employees to help them build the necessary skills to meet the fast pace of technology change.

The need to learn effectively and acquire the necessary knowledge becomes an important surviving skill for everyone. Learning will never stop – even after you finish your education in school. Your workplace and life is more demanding and creating challenges for you to learn quickly and apply the knowledge immediately.

According to the Association for Talent Development (ATD), the companies which provide formal training for their employees will have a 218% higher income per employee and a 24% higher profit margin when compared with those companies without the training. By summarizing the key finding of the industrial reports, it shows the average training hours for each employee is around 30 to 45 hours per year.

The pace of development in the world grows quicker and quicker, sometimes making global citizens run to follow it. Those who cannot follow the development will be left behind with frustration, fear, and anger. The digital divide and also the knowledge gap is widening for those who cannot access and master the technology of using the free but great internet resources.

As an educator, I believe knowledge can empower people and change lives. My life is proof of that, and my personal stories support my belief. In this chapter, I will empower you by sharing tips to help you become a professional learner, so you can prepare yourself and stand for the rapid change in the world by facing the challenge without fear.

THE PROFESSIONAL LEARNER'S THREE (3) CHARACTERISTICS

Usually, the less effective learner will believe that he or she is not so smart, so the learning performance is not satisfying. Is this a fact? Is there nothing that can be done to enhance the learners' performance for the intelligence level that is fixed? As an educator, I do not agree with this. I believe anyone can become a better and more professional learner if one can develop three characteristics. I am going to elaborate on the three points in detail.

A professional learner should have the following characteristics:

1. **THE PROACTIVE LEARNER**
2. Look for **STRUCTURE AND FRAMEWORK**
3. The **EXPERIMENTAL SPIRIT** – attitude to problems and failure

1. <u>THE PROACTIVE LEARNER</u>

The following chart summarizes the key concepts of a proactive learner:

Proactive Learner	Characteristic	Keywords / Concepts/ Tools	How to transform one into a proactive learner (external and internal forces: the learner, parents, educators, leaders, employers, HRD, L&D, the government, all can take action and support the learners' positive transformation).
	1.1 Ability to visualize the value or outcome caused by learning	Set clear objectives and achieve benefit-driven outcomes by using SMART	• See the value or outcome caused by the learning activity (helps build a stronger drive). • Take care of the psychological aspect as well, and not only focus on skill training.
	1.2 Learning without fear	Remove the fear with encouragement and recognition	• Add game or competition elements in the learning process and activities to improve the UX of learning, so you can enjoy the learning process.
	1.3 Make the learning process enjoyable	Create an entertaining learning experience by service design: UX, CX, gamification	• Compare and contrast different learning content and strategies to find one which suits your learning styles, pace, and requirements.

1.1 Ability To Visualize A Benefit-Driven Outcome Caused By Learning

The proactive learner means one will take an active role and responsibility in the learning process to achieve the best learning outcome. The best learner usually reacts proactively as he or she can see the value and the positive outcome caused by learning. On the other hand, a weaker learner usually reacts passively and lacks motivation for studying. If the learner cannot visualize or imagine the positive result caused by the learning activities, it will also affect the immediate learning performance, as you cannot enjoy the learning process.

Clear objective setting/ benefit-driven outcomes

I had an experience when delivering a drawing module to students who were majoring in music. The music students did not understand why they needed to study drawing. They cannot link up the learning and the benefits for their future career, which affects their learning attitudes and performance.

My strategy was to trigger the students' motivation by telling them that if they have a music show or performance on the stage, they may need to visualize their stage design and floor plan by drawing it – which is a more effective way than by verbal communication. It worked for those students who had an expectation of holding their own music performance but did not apply to those who wanted to become music engineers and worked backstage.

Educators have an important role to help learners to learn more proactively by triggering their motivation. Converting learners from a passive to a proactive learning mode will help them to learn better. This is just like a leader needing to create a clear vision for the followers, so everyone sees the light in the uncertainty, and are willing to walk forward.

1.2 Learning Without Fear

Fear and pressure are key obstacles which affect one's performance in general, especially in learning. Removal of fear and stress will absolutely help the learner to learn more effectively.

For most trainers, delivering the skills and content is the focus of learning; a normal trainer will not think it is their responsibility to take care of the psychological state of the learner. The implicit element, such as the pressure within the learner, will affect the whole learning performance.

Encouragement is powerful

Encouragement or recognition given by the expert or leader is a very powerful tool that helps to remove the fear and pressure, a key performance barrier. It accelerates the learner's transformation from passive to proactive learning mode.

STORY – Be Empathetic, Magic will happen!

When I started my MA course in the UK, I was stressed due to my dissatisfaction with my English level, and worried it would affect my overall academic performance. At that time, I needed to study a module called Broadcast Journalism, which required me to interact with different international students and to talk in front of the camera. The lecturer did one great thing which impressed and inspired me. It also removed my fear of using English to learn immediately in the first lesson.

What did the lecturer do? The lecturer invited all the international and local students to sit together in a circle, then asked us, "What was your fear that may affect your performance as a presenter in front of the camera?" My answer to her was my English standard. She sincerely replied to me, "I respect and appreciate every international student who is using English, which is not your mother tongue, to study. For me, I cannot do it! You know you are wonderful!"

She reassured all international students of their ability to learn using a foreign language, which helped me and other students build our confidence, removing our fear so that we could focus on learning and were able to enjoy the learning process.

During the training, delivering skills and knowledge is an important task, but there is a more important ritual or step before the learning starts. Helping the learners to remove an implicit element, such as the psychological barrier of fear and pressure, is very important to improve the learners' performance. An empathetic educator will be more powerful in teaching and can accelerate and improve the learners' performance.

1.3 Make The Learning Process Enjoyable By Creating A Stunning Learning Experience With Design Thinking, Gamification And UX

Recently, there are lots of design tools and frameworks to help industries and users to transform from a traditional model to meet the new challenge. There are lots of online resources, books, and workshops talking about these creative tools. The most famous and widely applied practices include design thinking, business model canvas, service design, user experience design, LEGO Serious Play, and gamification. All these practices can be applied to create an innovative learning experience and help learners to become a proactive learner, once they can enjoy the learning process and be engaged in the learning activities.

No matter if you are a parent, an educator, or a businessman, there will be people you care about who need to learn. How to help yourself or the people you care about to learn effectively and enjoy the learning process is important. You can take an active role in using the above tools to design new learning activities and to enhance any learners' performance.

2. FINDING STRUCTURE AND FRAMEWORK

A professional learner usually develops a habit of finding structure or framework within chaos, which will help one to understand the subject matter and learn quickly. How do you put this concept into practice and apply it in daily learning activities?

Let us say that you are given a brand new topic, and you need to learn it in a given timeframe. First, you can go to the internet, the library, or a bookshop, find the Best Sellers on the topic, especially the books written by experts in that field, published by the authorized publishers, or finding online reading with a higher search ranking. The learning can start with a quick scanning of the table of contents and the summary, in order to develop a clear and basic knowledge structure which can be expanded and subject to change later, once there is more information to flow in.

In the initial stages of learning a new topic, the learner does not need to read through the whole book immediately as there may be a time limitation. The learner can pick a chapter that seems useful or interesting, and within thirty minutes, they know whether they are connected with the author and enjoy his or her writing and presentation style.

Browsing quickly over a series of learning materials before digging deep into it, will help the learner develop the sense of distinguishing which resource is better, and worth the learner's time to devote the energy to study, but with less effort and better understanding of the topics.

2.1 Effective Learning With Well-Structured Reading And With Visual Hierarchy

Good learning materials usually have good structure as the content reflects the thinking structure and logistic pattern of the writer. Regardless of if it is online or a printed version, a reading with a well-structured, visual hierarchy supported by clear headers and sub-headers will enhance the learning effectiveness, as it shortens the learning time and effort to read and understand the topics. The learner should make an effort to locate such learning materials, as they have a higher readability and make scanning possible for readers.

2.2 Different Knowledge Structures Will Frame Understanding Differently

The knowledge structure is useful and functions like well-constructed furniture. Imagine it is a wardrobe with different spaces for categorizing the clothes according to the features and users' logic for using the clothes – such as size, colour, thickness, length, materials, functions, etc. This knowledge structure functions exactly like information architecture. Big winter clothes may be hung instead of putting inside a drawer, as the user may not be able to find it easily. Similar items sharing the same features should be grouped together so they are easier to locate.

A good framework or knowledge structure functions exactly like a well-designed wardrobe. It allows users to store and access their knowledge effectively. The framework of furniture will affect the behaviour and interaction with the clothes in the same way that the knowledge structure will affect the expandability and understanding of the knowledge, framing how one understands the world. That is why exploring different knowledge structures in different dimensions will be an important and effective way to expand the learner's learning capability and understand a topic effectively.

Locating reading materials written by experts in different fields, different cultures, timeframes, and media channels that talk about similar topics can expand the learner's breadth and depth of knowledge for that subject matter. The practice of comparing and contrasting different knowledge structures and finding common patterns or characteristics within different knowledge structures will help learners to find innovative elements and be inspired.

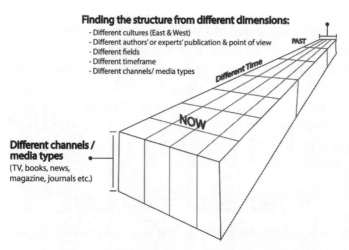

Finding the structure from different dimensions:
- Different cultures (East & West)
- Different authors' or experts' publication & point of view
- Different fields
- Different timeframe
- Different channels/ media types

PAST

Different Time

NOW

Different channels / media types
(TV, books, news, magazine, journals etc.)

Finding Consistent Knowledge Structure in Different Fields & Dimensions

3. <u>EXPERIMENTAL SPIRIT</u>

There is so much information around us, what can we believe and how can we prove the information is valid and trustable? For the professional learner, you can conduct social or online experiments to test your observations and your thoughts before you believe or embrace them.

There are many free online and internet resources for professionals to conduct their own experiments. The common practice, tools and theories include A/B test, data and social analytics tools, data-driven analysis, usability tests, ethnographic research, and guerrilla research. All these practices can help you to conduct research and experiments to determine if your observation or belief is valid or not.

An experimental mindset means the learner must be tough and positive to accept that problems and failures are common in the process of experimentation. Problems and failures are not something bad, but they help learners to evolve quickly as they reveal weaknesses, give hints for improvement, and finally lead us to success.

The world is full of uncertainty and changes quickly; sometimes, we are not sure which expert's advice or answers we should follow. With the affordable cloud services and abundant free resources developed by the developers, and the generous internet heroes, it has never been so easy and possible for global citizens to be successful by conducting experiments to understand the world and gain insight through data-driven evidence. The internet will be an exciting, interesting playground and lab for everyone to explore, evolve, and become excellent in your field.

ARE YOU READY TO FACE THE CHALLENGE?

A famous Asian proverb reflects a common Chinese belief which says, "There is a golden house within the books." Western culture shared a similar value, as Benjamin Franklin said, "An investment in knowledge pays the best interest."

We are on the road of a knowledge-based economy, and life-long learning will become mainstream culture. Government and Enterprise will continue to promote and support continuous learning to build a competitive workforce. If you want to get control of your life and career, and you do not want to be left behind, then you need to be a professional learner and empower yourself and the people you care about to close the knowledge gap around you.

About Daisy

Daisy Shuk Yin Ng is a graduate of Digital Graphic Communication from Hong Kong Baptist University and has an M.A. in Electronic-Journalism from the University of Sheffield (UK). She has rich working experience in both academic and commercial fields, which emphasize the application of interactive communication art and design. She never stops her evolution from a designer, and keep upskilling by enriching her knowledge in different fields such as technical development, user experience, digital marketing, SEM, SEO, data analytics and data science.

Observing people who want to be successful but fail to do so, makes Daisy feel the need to support them, using her expertise and experience. She feels the pain of citizens who struggle to survive by learning to reskill themselves to meet the global challenges in life and the workplace.

With over 20 years of experience in multimedia production, and tertiary education for art and design, Daisy understands the importance for bridging the knowledge gap between learning and teaching, and between content experts and target audiences.

Daisy has a broad knowledge base which covers different disciplines and the modules she taught – including interactive communication and customer experience, interactive information design, research studies in creative media, digital marketing and online advertising, user interface and user experience, digital graphics and visualization, figure drawing, semiotics, etc. Daisy has also led final year students to develop their graduation projects for web and apps since 2004.

Daisy participated in various multimedia and web projects which included digital TV, website development for Hong Kong-Zhuhai-Macau Bridge, and different companies' in-house websites. Her roles include content development, information architecture design and channel operation, providing consultation and advice to stakeholders, to ensure the project can meet professional standards and achieve clients' objectives.

Prior to joining the education industry, Daisy worked for internet service providers and publishers in Hong Kong. She supported both internal and external multimedia projects and performed many various roles including project coordinator, editor, designer, writer, and voice talent. She has been involved in designing educational projects for publishers such as Longman, Ling Kee and Oxford. Daisy was the author, project coordinator and writer for the guidebook, Photoshop CS 40 Hot Skills, which was published under the brand of *PC Weekly* (Hong Kong) in 2004.

Daisy upskills herself in search marketing (SEM, SEO), data science and analytics, which arms her with rational tools and metrics to measure the success of digital content and understand users' feedback in different purchasing stages. She targets becoming the top content strategist and educator who helps learners and clients to use the web and internet to be successful, as it is the most effective and affordable way for everyone to connect oneself with the world.

To connect with Daisy Shuk Yin Ng:
- daisyng5@gmail.com
- https://www.linkedin.com/in/daisy-ng-shuk-yin-71021627/

CHAPTER 9

WHY NOT ME?

BY AYO OLASEINDE

PART 1

Has the world seen the best of you? Do you have more to give? Is this it, you are maxed out, or do you have more in you to give?

I am Ayo Olaseinde, president of a global organization working in over fifty countries worldwide, with a turnover in hundreds of millions of dollars per annum. And my journey to success – from my humble beginnings sleeping on a friend's couch – started with asking the question, 'Why?' This is my story of how I came about asking the question, "Why? Why not me?" and, by the same token, "Why not you?"

Think about this. When we were children, we constantly asked our parents and teachers the question, "Why?"

You would get an answer, and then you would ask the question, "Why?" one, two, three, four, or five times. You asked, "Why?" until your parents and teachers got angry with you and told you to stop being silly. This then became the point where you realised that asking the "Why?" question is not a good thing to do.

Children are always asking the question, "Why? Why? Why?

Why?" They do it obsessively; they drill down to find the core answer.

This constant question, while simple, is one of the greatest ways children learn and grow. When we become adults, we stop asking the "Why? Why? Why?" question, and stop growing. As we drift through life, we tend to stop asking this simple yet powerful question. By re-introducing the question "Why?" into our daily lives, we can develop a better understanding of life, and learn to build a happier, more positive and successful way of life.

"Why?" is one of the most powerful questions you can ask yourself if you use it positively. For example, "Why are some people more successful than others?" "Why are some people happier than others?"

It took me many years to realise that nobody is better than you, but they might be doing something you are not doing yet? To develop my guide to your success, I will give you three things that separate successful people from others at the end of my chapter.

By constantly asking myself the question, "Why?" I have enjoyed tremendous success. For me, the moment which changed my life involved working as a casual labourer in a bakery. I started to ask myself the question, "Why? Why am I stuck in the life I am currently living?" This was my life at the age of twenty-four. Now, I am a successful businessman who has built an organisation that has turned over hundreds of millions of dollars through my past and current business ventures.

The question I am asking myself now is, "Why have I not reached one billion dollars yet?" Simply put, by re-introducing the question "Why?" into my life, I have been able to achieve tremendous success – both professionally and personally.

THE BAKERY

To share my own journey to building a happy and successful life, we turn to when I was a young man, aged twenty-four. I was working in the music business with my brother, Dele, and we were going to be successful in the music business.

However, it was the total opposite, nothing worked out and we lost the little money we had. I had hired a car and took it back on an empty tank of fuel. When I returned the car to the car hire firm, they gave me my £5 deposit, which I had left for the keys if I ever lost them.

I remember standing in the road after returning the car, saying to myself, "This is all I have… £5 to my name?" It was a rather low day for me. From here, I ended up sleeping on my friend Ellen's couch, and had to start over again. This failure led me to a job as a casual labourer, working in a bread factory.

Getting this job did not come easy. I had to stand in line outside the bakery with the other potential workers every day, hoping to get a day's work when demand was high—a truly humbling experience. I was never selected at first, but I kept coming back to the bakery door every day.

Eventually, I was picked by the foreman to work for the day. I worked very hard that day, and I was asked to come back the next day. I worked even harder the second day I was chosen and continued to work harder and harder every day I was selected, simply because I was willing to work hard and willing to learn. Eventually, the union workers became angry because the Manager was giving me all of the overtime hours. With redundancies at the bakery on the horizon, I needed to move on. I knew I could not continue to live with this sort of uncertainty as well as the low wage which came with the job. I desperately needed to make a change in my life.

In many ways, the seed for the need to change to a successful lifestyle was now planted in my head. So, you can see I was a wanderer and, when the redundancy pattern interrupted my life, it caused me to ask, "Why am I in this position? This cannot be my life, can it?"

In the beginning, I didn't have the money to take the bus to the bakery, so I would have to walk four miles, each way, every day. I walked at night to the bakery, getting there about 9 pm to start my shift at 10 pm. In time, when I started catching up with my finances, I began to take the bus. Not the entire way. Instead, I would continue to walk part of the journey so I could save twenty-four pence on the bus fare. During these walks, I would see people passing me in luxury cars – driving BMWs, Jaguars, and Mercedes. It was here that I started asking myself the question, "Why, Why Not Me? Why am I not one of the people driving a Mercedes or a Jaguar around town? What am I doing wrong, and where did it all begin to go wrong?" The "Why, Why Not Me?" questions were beginning to ferment in my head.

With the extra money I saved by walking part of the way, as well as the extra income which came with the extra shifts at the bakery when possible, I found other ways to save money. For instance, at the bakery, we were allowed to eat as much bread as we wanted. So, I would bring a bit of butter to work and feast on a simple lunch of freshly-baked bread and standard butter.

This added to my savings, which allowed me to get off my friend's couch, and into my own apartment once again. Whilst being a difficult and humbling period of my life, my experiences in the bakery helped me to begin my path to a successful and sustainable life.

In life, adversity although not appreciated, can be the best teacher.

During my time at the bakery, I asked myself, "Is this what God wanted or intended for me? Why not me? What do these successful people have that I do not have?" I finally reached the point in life where I was sick and tired of being sick and tired and something within me snapped and I asked the question, "Why, Why Not Me?" I am willing to learn, work hard and do whatever it takes, so long as it's ethical and honest.

So, I began on my path to get out of that situation, and never looked back. In a sense, I entered the "Why Factor", and continued to keep this simple yet powerful style of thought in my head at all times. I looked at my options. I had no qualifications, so I had a choice. I could go back to college, which was not an option, or go back to working in a factory, labouring, or find someone in a business that would train me. I already knew that direct sales was one of the few professions that takes people from all backgrounds and trains them.

I answered an advert and got a job in Direct Sales. This position offered me the opportunity for tremendous growth and personal development.

Joining the world of sales, while constantly asking myself the question "Why" has given me a tremendous amount of professional and personal success; *remember, nobody is better than you, but they might be doing something you are not doing yet.*

From those humble beginnings, I built a very successful business that ended up turning over 40 million pounds before I semi-retired. I was then head-hunted from the USA to start a new business in the UK from scratch.

After fourteen years, I was made president of the company worldwide. As you can imagine, my life is very different now than it was during the bakery days.

I tell you this story not simply to impress you, but to impress upon you that anybody can do it if you are prepared to do the things successful people do. Success is something that can be learnt and achieved; it is not a gift. You have to start believing in yourself and asking, "Why not you?" Now, can you give me one reason why you should not be successful?

Never ever, ever question your ability, but always question your performance!!!

PART 2

That is why I wrote my book called, *Have You got the Why Factor?* Welcome to the Why Factor! My system for achieving a healthy, successful, and positive lifestyle is nothing new. Instead, the Why? Factor relies on a characteristic within us that has been around since the beginning of time, asking the "Why?" question: "Why not me? Why not you?"

The Why Factor is not a system for immediate success. Instead, the Why Factor journey is a process of continuous improvement. You see, there is no upper limit of success in the Why Factor, you will always be striving to become more successful and having fun doing so. For this reason, the Why Factor is more of a dynamic way of living.

The 'Why?' question you ask yourself today will be very different when compared to the 'Why?' questions you will ask yourself in ten years. Remember that improvement within the Why Factor is a continuous, life-long process. In other words, success is not a gift or luck, *it can be learnt.*

Just because you may have been dealt a bad hand in life doesn't mean that you cannot turn your life around and win in the game of life. You were born to succeed. The only way to succeed is that you must want to learn and change. And asking the question, "Why not me?" is the beginning. The challenge is not how good the teacher is, it is how good the student is! Are you a good student willing to listen, learn and apply?

I learned from Brain Tracy many years ago that there are three elements in success:

1) Decide exactly what you want in life.
2) Decide the price you have to pay to get it.
3) Pay the price!

Most people want success but are not willing to pay the price. Are you prepared to pay the price? That's why you have to 'Pay it Forward'. Pay first, then you get the benefits later. Food for thought, when you see anyone successful, it is important to realise how many hours they have invested in their profession to perfect it. We think it is talent!

I have spent many years studying successful people *and* failures. Yes, I studied both. I learnt to copy the successful people and avoid the mistakes failures make. What I would like to share with you are my findings and three keys to success. They are simple but not easy:

A) **Attitude** - All successful people have a positive attitude, believe in themselves, their business, and are optimistic about the outcome of their business.

B) **Work Rate** - They work very hard. Relentless hard work is the best substitute for talent. They might be lazy when they are rich, but when building, they gave it everything they had.

C) **Skill** - They master their skill in whatever profession they are in. They are committed to excellence. Just being good is not good enough.

Michael Jordan said, practice, practice, practice, till it is instinctive. Like I said, take any successful person and study them. They have distilled their success down to Attitude, Work Rate and Skill.

Never question your ability; always question your performance.

That's why my question to you is: "Why not you?"

"Why??????"

Are you prepared to pay the price for success or the price of failure?

Either way you are paying!!!

About Ayo

Ayo Olaseinde's father is Nigerian, his mother German, and he was born in the UK, what a great combination...

Ayo was six weeks old when his parents took him to Nigeria. He was brought up there and came back to England when he was 18 years old with no qualifications. Today Ayo Olaseinde is a successful businessman who has built an organisation that has turned over $500 million worth of merchandise through his past and current business ventures.

During Ayo's first few years in the UK, he drifted about, and dropped to his lowest point when he ended up homeless sleeping on a friend's couch, with just a case full of clothes. He had to get a job, so he walked four miles every day to stand outside the bakery to hopefully get a night's casual labour which would pay $10 a night. Because he worked very hard, he was regularly selected as a casual labourer.

One day, whilst walking to the bakery, Ayo asked himself, "Is this my life? Is this what God wanted or intended for me?" Just then, a Mercedes with a family in it drove past. He looked at them and said to himself. "Why me? Why not me? What are they doing that I'm not doing?" That blew his mind. If he stayed at that factory, he would not be able to succeed; that was the day he decided to find another way.

Ayo answered an advert for a job in Direct Sales. This position offered the opportunity for tremendous growth and personal development. He started at the bottom, and within two years, he was running his own branch and built one of the largest Distributorships in the UK, turning over £40,000,000. He ended up running part of the UK operation before deciding to semi-retire.

Ayo was then head-hunted by a 60-year-old American company that operated in 40 countries to start up a new business in the UK. He started on his own, using skills and techniques he had acquired, and built the UK market and expanded into Europe, Africa, and the Middle East, becoming the fastest-growing region with just under 100 outlets and earning the title of 'Most Valuable Life Changer' eight years later.

Ayo then became the president of Saladmaster UK, the first entity to be established outside the USA in 70 years. And in 2018, he was made Global President, again the first global president outside of the USA in over 50 plus countries, and the business continues to grow using the same philosophy and skills and techniques he acquired.

So Ayo began his path to get out of that situation in the beginning, and never looked back. In a sense, he continued to keep this simple yet powerful style of thought of asking "Why not me?" in his head at all times.

Ayo says:

"Never question your ability, just question your performance.
Success can be learnt. We can teach you!
Nobody is better than you!
Anything is possible if you believe and work hard!!!!
Be the change in your life!"

CHAPTER 10

MOVING TO AMERICA FROM CANADA

BY EDWARD L. ROTH, CFP®

I can relate to Ben Huh's video on YouTube in a very personal way. I also am an immigrant. At age 9, I moved from Tofield, Alberta, Canada, where I was born, to Northwest Ohio, and I like to say my parents came along. My grandfather, Valentine Roth, moved from Milford, Nebraska, to Tofield, Alberta, Canada, in 1910 with his family – which included my father Reuben, who was three years old at the time of the move. My grandfather and his brother Nick Roth bought several sections of prairie land in that area. As you no doubt know, a section of land is 640 acres. At that time, it was a major undertaking, because they did not have modern heavy equipment to break the prairie, so it could be farmed. They used mostly horses. However, they did have a Hugh one-cylinder tractor that burned kerosene. As a very young child, I still recall them breaking the prairie soil about a mile from where we lived because of the loud sound of this tractor. It sounded like this: Poom, Poom.

During the winter, my dad and other young men would travel by train back to Milford, Nebraska, to visit relatives, and to get out of the cold winter as there was not much to do on the farm because the harvest was over until spring. I have also suspected that while in Nebraska, they may have been on a lookout for a wife because that is where he met my mother. They corresponded by mail for a year and then got married and moved to Alberta. My grandfather told my dad that he and my mother could establish a ¼-section farm of his land. There were no buildings on the ¼ section, so the first building they built was a granary. They wanted to make sure they had a place to store the grain just in case there was an early winter. They lived in the granary until the house was built. In the spring of 1941, they decided they would move to America in the fall. My sister and I had mixed emotions about this move because we would miss being with our cousins and friends. We had so many pleasant memories of the many good times together. Then my dad tried to encourage us by talking about the expanded opportunities in America.

I also remember my grandmother not being happy about the move. My dad once told her, "…but they have paved roads were we are moving to." Her response was, "That is nothing, in Heaven, we will have streets paved with gold."

I still remember the night before we left, we were at my grandmother's house saying goodbye by standing in a circle holding hands and singing this song: "Walking Along Life's Road One Day." When I sing this song, it still is emotional for me even at my advanced age.

My parents thought they would have no trouble moving to America with their two children, my 6-year-old sister and I, a 9-year-old, since my parents were both born in America. However, because my sister and I were born in Canada, this presented a problem at the U.S. border. My parents did not have birth certificates for their children. Consequently, they would not let us enter America. We were traveling by train, so my parents had to unload our belongings at the border.

The authorities called the recorder of birth certificates in the city of Edmonton (the capital of the province of Alberta), to verify that we were indeed the children of our parents. However, the authorities at the border needed to have an original copy of the birth certificates and would not let us enter America. Of course, in 1941, there were no faxes or scanners. So my dad arranged to have the birth certificates issued and put on the next train. I have no idea how he paid to have the certificates issued or paid to have them shipped on the next train, as there was no such thing as credit cards then. He may have used Western Union.

The next challenge for my parents was where we would sleep until the next train arrived with the certificates. The authorities gave permission for our family to stay in the jail together as a family until the certificates arrived in the next day or two. So my claim to fame is that for my first two days in America, my family and I slept in jail. As a result, I now carry a small copy of my Birth Certificate with me.

I know it was a relief for my parents when we boarded the train for Milford, Nebraska. We stayed with relatives in Milford for about a week. One interesting side note is that my mother would cut my hair and my father's with a hand clipper, because we had no electricity in Canada. So my mother said, I am going to have Edward get a real haircut from a barber. Even though I was nine years old, I had never been in a barbershop and when the barber sat me down in the barber chair and turned on the electric clipper, it scared me half to death with the buzzing. It brought tears to my eyes.

While in Milford, my dad bought a 1935 Chevrolet to drive to Ohio to meet with a neighbor we had in Alberta that moved to Ohio a few years before we did. I still remember him bragging in Canada how nice Ohio was, and that the grass was always green the year around. As a boy, that was hard to believe because of all the snow we had in Alberta. Well, I soon found out that the grass may be green all winter in Ohio, but for a few months, it is under the snow.

I recall driving from Milford, Nebraska, to Ohio. We would not sleep in hotels, and there were very few motels, but we slept in the car in village parks. We also very seldom ate in a restaurant. My mother would go to the grocery store and buy a loaf of bread and a pound of sliced baloney. She then made sandwiches for us. To say we were poor is an understatement. Although my sister and I did not feel poor, our parents did their best to fill our needs.

After we settled in a bit in Ohio, along came December 7, 1941, when Japan bombed Pearl Harbor. I am sure this brought more uncertainty to my parents. Why am I sharing this with you? It is to illustrate that being an immigrant is not for the faint-hearted. It takes courage. Perhaps that is why many immigrants are good entrepreneurs. They are willing to step out and take a chance.

My parents instilled a spirit of a positive attitude, and I will take the liberty of sharing some of their sayings:

- Our attitude is our personal boomerang to the world — Whatever we throw out will come back.
- You will reap what you sow.
- If wishes were horses, beggars would ride.
- Things are never as good as they seem, and things are never as bad as they seem.
- It's Not the Wind; it's the Set of the Sails.
- Can't fell in the ditch and died in the poor house.
- The darker the night, the brighter the light.
- My mother once told me, "Cheer up things could be worse." I took her advice and cheered up. Sure enough, things did get worse. Keep smiling!
- Over time, good will always overcome evil.
- The time is always right to do what is right.
- Never look down on anyone unless you are helping them up.
- Keep on the Sunnyside.

So let us all not be too hard on the immigrants, they are only trying to improve their station in life. They also can bring value to our country.

Let us all so live that when we come to die
even the undertaker will be sorry.
~ Mark Twain

Endnotes:

(1). *Raymond James is not affiliated with Northwest Investment Co., O'Artic Investment Co., Roth, Britsch, Dickman, Inc. or Investment Planning Associates

(2). The information contained in this book does not purport to be a complete description of the securities, markets, or developments referred to in this material. The information has been obtained from sources considered to be reliable, but we do not guarantee that the foregoing material is accurate or complete. Any information is not a complete summary or statement of all available data necessary for making an investment decision and does not constitute a recommendation. Any opinions of the chapter authors are those of the chapter author and not necessarily those of RJFS or Raymond James. Expressions of opinion are as of the initial book publishing date and are subject to change without notice. Certified Financial Planner Board of Copyright © 2019

(3). All Rights Reserved ISBN.

(4). Dedication: The Purpose and goal of writing this chapter is to be a source of encouragement to my children, grandchildren, and great-grandchildren and dedicate it to my wife and partner these past 65 years. Without her loving support, it would have been impossible to have a rewarding life that I have lived. This book is dedicated to Mildred L Bontrager Roth, who is the love of my life.

(5). Certified Financial Planner Board of Standards Inc. owns the certification marks CFP®, CERTIFIED FINANCIAL PLANNER™, CFP® (with plaque design) and CFP® (with flame design) in the U.S., which it awards to individuals who successfully complete CFP Board's initial and ongoing certification requirements. Securities offered through Raymond James Financial Services, Inc. – Member FINRA/SIPC. Investment advisory services are offered through Raymond James Financial Services Advisors, Inc.

About Edward

Edward L. Roth, CFP®, Branch Manager, is a registered principal, a registered options principal, a licensed insurance agent and a registered investment advisor representative. Ed worked in consumer finance for 15 years prior to his 27 years of experience in the financial field.

Ed is president of Northwest Investment Co., general partner of O'Artic Investment Co., and president of Roth, Britsch, Dickman, Inc. DBA: Investment Planning Associates, an independent practice.*

Ed Roth is a CERTIFIED FINANCIAL PLANNER™ professional, a member of the Institute of CERTIFIED FINANCIAL PLANNERS™, and a past board member of the local chapter of the International Association of Financial Planners. Ed is a graduate of the New York Institute of Finance and Investment Training.

Ed is also a past Vice-President of Ethics for the board of the Northwest Ohio FPA (Financial Planning Association) and the author of *The Twelve Steps To A Meaningful Life.*

Ed and his wife, Millie, reside in rural Archbold, Ohio, and are the proud parents of four children, ten grandchildren and four great-grandchildren.

Ed's office is located at 103 Main Street, Pettisville, OH 43553.

*Raymond James is not affiliated with Northwest Investment Co., O'Artic Investment Co., Roth, Britsch, Dickman, Inc. or Investment Planning Associates.

CHAPTER 11

IN SEARCH OF JOY
"WHERE TIME IS KING AND QUEEN, AND WE PLAY TOGETHER."

BY ANTÓNIO CHANOCA

I believe in a world where we do not have to give up our life in order to make a living.

That world is possible—today. But it is a very different kind of world that we see when we look around. Why? Not because we want this world to be like this, at least surely not the majority of us. But because, in a way, we "started on the wrong foot," and we now need to change the stepping. It is not easy, but it is far, far more possible than we think.

I am far from having all the answers. Actually, I am far from having all the questions—which would be a fantastic start to begin with. However, I do have two things: an unshakable conviction that living in an enjoyable, livable world is possible, and an insurmountable will to decisively contribute to making it happen.

As I said, I am far from having all the answers, solutions, or ways forward. But none of the great explorers had those when they set foot ashore to explore the land or sail the seven seas. On the contrary, they were, without exception, facing the greatest challenges of their lives precisely because of the absence of certainty, as well as the absolute proven right way. If the way was proven, it would, by definition, have been crossed by someone before them, the anti-definition of exploring, as someone before had done it. So, the fact that we have no certainties of "how"shall not prevent us from moving forward. The destination is far too important not to be attempted, and the way is far too rich not to be enjoyed.

The challenge is now to give a glimpse of "how" this can be done in a clear set of conditions: a short enough way so that people keep on reading until it starts to make sense, and going until they exert an "elational" attraction to be part of it—truly a part of it.

I will, therefore, risk to state the case of how this can be done in a "movie trailerish way." I will supply enough information so that one gets the sense of the narrative, without the time for details or getting the full picture as yet. As such, let me go and start setting the stage.

In biological terms, humankind only has two needs in order to stay alive—two and two alone. They are shelter and nutrition. I am not saying that one's life is complete without another set of important ingredients for one's existence. Elements such as belonging, bonding, acceptance, and love are needed in the very first instance for a balanced and joyful life. I not only have no doubt about them first hand, and in my own experience, I find them fundamental for an enjoyable life to be lived.

Personally, I do not want or wish to live without them, and with that said, I firmly affirm that all those emotional elements are of great relevance for a fulfilled life. But my first, my very first point is a different one: what does it take for a human being to stay biologically afloat? Two and two things alone: shelter and nutrition. And I have, for simplicity, divided these two into five categories:

1. Nutrition can be divided into three: air, water, and food.
2. Shelter, we will divide into two: mobile shelter, which we call clothing, and fixed, that we call housing.

So, let's pause for a second here. What have I said so far? I said that the world must evolve in a way that human beings do not have to systematically sacrifice their lives in order to make a living. I said that I believe that is not only desirable, as it is needed. And also, it is possible. (How it may be possible is what we will address more in-depth later, in another opportunity to deepen this chapter's content.) I also said that regardless of the fact that the emotional elements in our human lives are of extreme importance, I suggest that we begin focusing on the "mechanical" element of our existence as humans. And that is the biological critical few without which we won't make it, "till the next day."

I have identified those as nutrition and shelter, and I have for simplicity made five elements explicit: air, water, and food in the nutrition corner, and clothes and housing in the shelter corner. This is what I have said so far. Now, before we proceed, I have a question. Is this possible? Is it possible that everyone may have access to nutrition and shelter in a dignified way and not physically suffer from the absence of it, in today's world? Here is my undoubted answer: HECK, YES!!!

… More on the how, later on; not extensively, as one chapter would not allow it, but at least have a glimpse of the possibilities.

I have identified what I call the Core Needs, above. Now, what comes next are what I designate as enablers.

Let me reinforce that as a matter of simplicity, I am still leaving behind the emotional elements of Life—all the sublime feelings of comradery, belonging, appreciation, friendship, deep partnership, contribution, are definitely a fundamental "undiscardable" part of all of this. But please bear with me on the "mechanics" approach of the whole thing, before we move on to the "humanics" side of it all.

Once that we have identified the Core Needs, let's now talk about what I call the Enablers. As the name suggests, enablers are like levers—everything that in a way amplifies potential, power. In some instances, they amplify power, sometimes in orders of magnitude immensely high; in others, they perform tasks that were simply not possible for the human condition *per se*. Regardless of what they do, I will divide them into three categories, or types: know-how, machinery, and infra-structures.

We will later talk about all of this in detail. But let me give you a fast tour of what I am talking about here. Enablers are part of what humankind has developed in order to make our life easier. I will offer a few examples of how we can look at all of these in order to make easier a sense of an immense world.

Know-how: Everything that we "know" from a "cause-and-effect" perspective, or a physical sense. From chemical interactions to the laws of physics, all engineering knowledge, is part of this. Also, part of this is the element of what is called "social sciences," that without the same levels of "exactness" of the "mathematical" sciences, they too account for a significant part of know-how. If I wanted to pick up a word that could possibly encompass all the elements meant by the "know-how," that word could be "awareness." If I were to get really bold about it, and really want a word big enough where all in this realm would fit, I will then call it... Consciousness. If you come across an even "bigger bag" on this front, please send me an e-mail and share it with me.

Although far from everything is said in the area of the "know-how"/"awareness"/"consciousness" Enablers, a rough idea (even if only a very rough one) has been provided. So, what else is there in the realm of the Enablers? I also did mention machinery and infrastructures. Let's pick one of them and talk about machinery.

As machinery, I am considering a very broad sense of elements. I will actually "abuse" the term "machinery" to include all that is an extension of human ("physical") ability, or a "mechanical" enhancement of it. It gets easier if we offer examples. A wrench, a hammer, a screwdriver: none of these are "machines" per se, but for the sake of simplicity, I include them all and like-tools in the set of "machinery." On the other hand, an internal combustion engine, an electricity-generating turbine, or a capsule of a spacecraft are all equally in the "machinery" bucket.

Let's, therefore, consider Machinery enablers to be every human-made technology that "makes life easier" and/or make "impossible feats possible." You get the point. We will go far deeper into the "machinery enablers" in other possibilities where details can be revealed and explored in greater detail.

We are left with the third (and last for now) type of Enabler initially mentioned: in a very light way, introductory only, I have referred to "know-how" and "machinery." Let's now take a look at "Infra-Structures" as Enablers.

The first thing to say about "infrastructures" is that they are SYSTEMS. And as such, a lot of them, actually ALL of them, encompass… machinery! But as infrastructures, we are referring to the systems themselves and to what they provide in global terms, as opposed to what each individual part (or "machine") produces or stands for. In a way, machines "produce things," infrastructures "satisfy needs." Not necessarily like this, we can argue, but, again, you get the idea. Let's further explore the notion of infrastructures so that we get a clearer idea of what is meant.

First, let's start by identifying an array of areas with infrastructures as enablers. We use railways, road/land communications, ports/vessels, airports/air travel, as examples of physical transport infrastructure. Then, there are internet servers, telecoms, antennas, and TV stations, as examples of telecommunication infrastructure. And we use hospitals, ambulances, clinics, healthcare centers, pharmaceutical companies, and pharmacies, as the backbone of a (material) healthcare system.

Here we start to see that there is a fundamental web of systems and players interconnected in order to "make happen" a "few" types of things. What things? Our life on the planet. And this is where this text can get really exciting. If we pose the right question, or better yet, the right set of questions, then we may find ourselves dreaming and designing the world where we ought to be, the world where we can, may and must live, and the world where we don't have to give up our lives in order to make a living. Here is where we can and will be ourselves, enjoy ourselves, and grow and evolve as a species. A world where contribution and enjoyment walk (or shall I say DANCE!) hand in hand in a beautiful, inclusive for the whole AND inspiring for the self, Platform of Co-Creation will emerge and strive. With no "ism's." Just Beings.

Great! Sounds Great! But also seems quite "utopian," right... I mean, where do we start?

Well, two things on that line; first, let's add the "yet." I'll explain what I mean. "U" in Greek means the opposite of what comes after it, and "topos" means "place." So, something that is "Utopos" means "place-not" or no place. Precisely. Let's add the "yet" so it reads "no place yet." Sure! We are here – to remove the "U". About a bit more than just a century ago, let me give you a lot of "Utopias": cars, airplanes, computers, electricity, plastic, credit cards, nuclear power, submarines, space rockets, satellites, mobile phones, and the list goes on endlessly. Any utopic stuff, today, in the sentence before? None! All are here! All "possible"! All "true"! We all get the point. Utopian would now be to imagine a world without them. Well, this is one of the questions, at the beginning of this paragraph, about sounding great but looking utopic. Ticked, for now, I believe.

The second was, where do we start?

The answer is very simple. We start by answering that question.

Depending on the perspective, we can choose to say that "a lot still has to be done," or we can say, "a lot has already been done." Or we can choose to say something else: both-and. I choose that, as I have a Portuguese attraction to Paradox, and to thrive in it.

Indeed, a lot needs to be done. And I do believe that in the Mentality bit, this is where we need to carve out a lot of the next foundations. This is where the "Humanics" of humankind needs to start jumping on board. Beyond the "How" (because as they say, "where there is a will, there is a way"), the "Why" plays a definite role here.

Here is what I believe...

I believe that it is possible, for starters. Or at least that it is "potentially possible," which is a great start and a pleonasm in itself. If enough people may see it and want to make it happen, it will be made.

Imagine we design it. Imagine we design a "full-scale territory-based" playground and ask: "What's possible?" What's possible to do here? What if we channel the best part of us into building it, into making it happen? What if we put all automation possible to work for the two major needs in its five forms so that we end physical suffering from the absence of air, water, food, clothes, and shelter?

What if we put all vertical farming and 3D printing "know-how" in an "infrastructure of machinery" that caters to the whole basic needs of an African Country? Take Cape Vert, as an example, where I personally have some friends, and surely a design attempt can be accomplished. What if we here win the Core Needs battle, offer a "real life" example, and people get enthusiastic about it and dare to dream more and to try more? What if, for example, we can evolve the Country to a full-energy autonomy scenario, hydrogen-based, which, let's be honest here, cannot be that far-fetched in a territory full of sun, with lots of wind and surrounded by water!!!

Here and now we only have time to give a glimpse of the "mechanics" of all of this. But the last few sentences in the previous paragraph do really offer a notion where "Humanics" also can kick in. The 'mega' process of accomplishing this can be divided into infinite action bits of local, regional, individual and groups of all sorts.

Can you imagine the Phenomenal Orchestra of bonding, partnering, love, despair, hope, sufferance, joy, longanimity, passion and all feelings and emotions that the "Humanics" side of Life has to offer and live? Although fundamental, the nature of this short chapter does not allow us time/space, here and now, to delve deeply into any of that. Surely, in a fully-dedicated book, it will.

The Future is, I believe, a combination of a Social Media network aiming at Real World transformation and improvement – a "Mega Real Life Video Game." It can, and it probably will, be done.

We have an infrastructure with so many elements in existence on this Planet. (Some of them are at an ecological cost that is no longer sustainable—actually they never were, and must change, will change! But that too, is a different conversation.) As I was saying, we have "infrastructured" the World with a lot of "easiers of life," including roads, railways, telecom copper cables, and later antennas. But there are far more other mega infrastructures: water on pipes at home, as well as sewer networks, electricity production and transport for thousands of kilometers/miles. And the same with oil and gas. And so, so-o many other things…!

Why could we not 'infrastructure' the way we produce food in a similar way? In a way where local needs are totally catered for. Vertical farming is one simple example, today it is a proven, viable, concrete reality. And there is farming automation too. And there are so many others. The same with housing. Why not 3D printing of housing for everyone without a roof? Sure, yes, it's possible and doable. A roof over the heads with dignity for everyone.

We must create the Vision. We must start somewhere. Is it possible? Definitely! Not because I say so, but because it is highly desirable, greatly needed and the technology is there. It is HERE, TODAY!!! We must get our act together and have a combination of political power along with people action.

We must develop different sources and interconnected notions of a common livable future. The lines presented in books such as *The Donut Economy* from Kate Raworth, at a Macro level. The notion of the "Post-Capitalist and Post-Communist" values creation matrix of the For-Benefit Companies, where REAL purpose meets private initiative for a livable world, at the Micro level. We have examples of world leaders amiably challenging the *status quo*. Take Jacinda Arden, in New Zealand, as one example. Many people want it and many people need it. I do believe to the very last drop of my blood that we can, we should, we must and we will do it! Start it.

A lot needs to deepen. But we must start somewhere. We are ready, and we are eager to *Pay It Forward* in search of Joy!

In the well-known quotation from Goethe, he said, "Whatever you think you can do, or believe you can do, begin it. Action has Magic, Grace and Power in it." ☺

About António

People and Organizational Development have been António Chanoca's professional Ecosystem for the past 25 years.

Having studied Economy and Management, António chose to work in Organizational Development and Behavioral Training for the first part of his work life. Experiential learning, Leadership and Sales Training were his initial professional portfolio. António worked for the company that represented Brian Tracy in Portugal for several years, and was Master Trainer in "New Psychology of Sales" and "Maximum Achievement."

In 2000, António developed his own consulting company, later co-founding the FLOW Group—represented now on four continents. Over the years, António Chanoca has worked with thousands of people in hundreds of organizations and dozens of countries. Currently in FLOW, António serves on the Board, as well as being a Senior Consultant and managing global accounts.

Combined with university studies, António was President of AIESEC. Those extraordinary times really germinated the seeds that later on would blossom in different stages and places in the realm of Social Innovation. António engaged with a series of movements and organizations, of which The Chaordic Alliance, World Social Forum, Planetwork, Friendly Favors, The Fourth Sector Initiative, River Simple and ReFood were among the most relevant. His associates are a group of like-minded and like-hearted people that has kept growing over the years with a strong general alignment in purpose, turning contacts into significant friendship bonding.

In line with what has been mentioned before, António's energy and passion are devoted to contributing to "a world where we don't have to give up our lives in order to make a living." Initiatives where technology accompanies the humanistic need for a world that is meaningful and livable for us all, are core to his current choices and courses of action. It's his belief that we all need to work on a new "world value creation model" that does not exhaust the biological and emotional balance both of the planet and of humankind. We have the phenomenal challenge and glorious opportunity to re-invent the value creation chain of the world, in a way where no "isms" take over.

In this context, António sees himself as a "Neo Generalist." As such, his interests encompass a vast array of subjects, from vertical farming and food production to automation in general, digital fabrication, circular economy, sustainable mobility, access to clean water and sanitation, not leaving behind political voice and freedom, education and health, to mention a critical few. From exploring Kate Raworth's concept of the "Donut Economy" to implementing organizations inspired in the Fourth Sector's combination of social-purpose and self-sustainability, we must address social and economic change in large-scale terms and fast-paced action.

António was born in Setúbal, Portugal, where we can have the best *peixe assado* in the world! He speaks Portuguese, English and Spanish, participated in TEDx Setúbal in 2018, and currently lives close to Lisbon. António is a believer in simplicity and love, has a passion for nature, exploring, traveling, water, reading and likes to have fun with Amigos.

Contact information for António:
- LinkedIn: António Chanoca | LinkedIn
- Twitter: @amchanoca
- Instagram: António Chanoca | Instagram

CHAPTER 12

LOVE OF FAMILY IS A BLESSED THING
A TRIBUTE TO DAD AND MUM

BY JULIE MEATES

Time-honored messages tugged at her heart. While she traveled extensively living in many places, she came to see that home is where the love is. While many people searched the world over, she came to see that the love of family is one of life's greatest blessings. This impermeable fact helps create a foundation for the next generation to build on, for we all come from one – in its many guises and disguises, whether on the refugee borders or the streets of London, from a small village at the top of Everest or a capital city on the tip of the world. We are all searching for the elixir of life, not worldly fame. In the inner sanctum of the soul, we search for love and happiness. She was a lucky one, born into a humble home with the ingredient: the power of a simple and loving upbringing. Within it, there are gifts amidst life's challenges. Materialism was not the name of the game, but the simple treasures of love, smiles, joy, faith, laughter, and having fun together.

She opened the small green box that sat on the shelf by the photos. She'd never really taken much notice of it before. The lid popped off easily. Life these days had become way too complicated. While opening, she remembered the simplicity. Keep it simple, he would say. The KISS principle had become elusive, like the shifting sands of time. Something sparkled inside, catching a filament of light. Was it one of his mother's? She hadn't noticed it before. Small and delicate. Was it a reminder? He was a man who kept his life in order. There was no chaos. Folded inside was a tiny piece of paper with a simple message. Even crossed out words paid forward convey love. "I know the last years have been hard, but let me assure you, they do get easier as years go on, and you will have to smell the roses. You are a very kind and loving person."

Beside the green box lay the pink flower. *"Thanks for being there for all of us at a difficult time."* The pink flower of kindness that grows despite the challenges, keeping people in the pink through love and compassion; kindness beautifies, and like the mandarin tree when cultivated, produces fruit. It can help someone when they feel ground down. Lend a helping hand. Be the change.

Kindness makes our homes paradise on earth. For life, the most precious gift from God is family. The family is the sweet fruit of love. Try to make it better, not bitter. Help a garden flourish. The scent of a flower always stays in the hand that gives. Kind acts matter. What comes from one's hand, heart and mouth can heal, help, hurt, or harm.

If we only had time. When a parent passes from one world to the next, grief provides a space to reflect on our mortality and life. What is the purpose? We have time for this again with this pandemic in our history. You never know when your number is up. Treat everyone with kindness like it is your last. What is important?

Coffins lay with no one there, unlike our Dad, who had hundreds there.

So here goes, back in time.

The intensity of the pain of the prognosis so painful; that one feels like you could explode inside. Some reach for the bottle or solace on their own. To shift the pain gnawing deep inside: chose kindness. On this challenging Easter when death looms large as life, she dropped hundreds of Easter eggs in letterboxes, until the pain did subside. Before Easter morn in lockdown, hot cross buns, nuts, Easter eggs treat. Kindness in the treelined street.

A sorrow shared is a sorrow halved. A problem shared is a problem solved. As playwright George Bernard Shaw said, "A happy family is but an *earlier* Heaven." Happy family – pass it on. God gave you a family, so you may learn to love others.

His head lay softly on the pillow. *Tears flow down her face; she lay softly by his side. I don't want you to leave me.* "I love you" were the final words; 50 years of lasting memories. A heart afraid to cry is a heart afraid to love. If you die peacefully, you loved and were loved, and so he was. The poignancy in the silence of the moment touched her heart in ways unknown—she felt as though he was present – his spirit soaring like a seagull—and in the silence of the space was the power of love. He died at home with his family's care. They made mistakes. I've had a happy life, he whispered. For that, not many can say. Endearments from grandchildren sat at the end of his bed, whose measure of a person is best described by their words: "I love you, Nana and Granddad." Thank you for showing love in the good times and the bad.

It's their anniversary. We reflect upon those that we know. Born in one of the most inhospitable landscapes, one of the southernmost cities on this Earth in the City of Water and Light; the southern lights mixed with water, driving rain in high wind, meets the snow.

A small boy disembarks from the train, alongside his mother

and siblings. *It was pre-World War II and their marriage was over.* In this time, these conditions were unseen. No solo parent beneficiary, but hard work, the only answer he would know. Put your head upon my shoulder, care for you, I will. Look after mothers. Respect and be kind, for it is actions that speak louder than words.

> *A year later, in the country, down a partially-graveled road arrived their child number three. Her father's village in Ireland faced famine, war, and poverty. A place of timeless wonder, within the austere, cold climate, grows the strongest tree. A deep inner desire for a loving family, or community, helping others and serving humanity. Hobnail boots and up at 4 am to milk the cows, or pulling turnips from frost-cold ground.*

Together from this hardy climate, her Mum and Dad made a mighty team. Their eldest daughter was born smiling, in this humble landscape on a farm in a small community, where dreams come true. Life was simple and loving. As parents, they were present. Always there to lift our burdens.

From horses to ride, geese, sheep, pigs, cattle, vegetables home-grown, we were healthy and happy and never alone. Simple kindness shown to neighbors, families, friends, and community resources, for that we are glad. Ablution block was down the garden path where the man in the moon did light the cold wintery way. Be yourself. There is no one else like you. Be the best that you possibly can. Learn it from nature. Look after the Earth. Imagine if a sheep tried to become a horse. What a crazy world this would be. Don't compare yourself with others. There is no one in the world like you. No individual cell phones, or iPad, touch rather simple, loving human touch; party lines shared telephones in the community, not-party lines shared drinking down the High Street. Stars in the sky they could gaze, not iPhone clutch, the latest craze. Cloud formation in the sky and you looked people in the eye.

Neighbors cared, people spoke. Don't talk about someone behind their back. Southern hospitality filled the cold night air; inside their home, there was love in their heart, a big smile and family did care. If a job's worth doing, it's worth doing well. "Always need to leave the place better than when you found it," especially people. Like a praetorian guard or sergeant major protecting from the battle, and clean up our mess or like a shepherd watching your flock with a mission to raise a happy, healthy family. If you have got a problem, fix it. Thanks for teaching the great lesson on defusing a potentially volatile situation. Make a decision and do not argue in front of the children. Thank you for seeing our potential, giving us many opportunities, always confident we could be No 1, keeping us grounded. "Get off your high horse." Don't think you're better than anyone else. Like Pope Francis, do not end the day without making peace. Do not leave the house angry, without a hug, as you never know when your number's up.

Homemade baking dropped in a reused tin, and the rhythm of life was to the tune of nature. Children worked side by side, chattering happily – sometimes silence. Talk less, listen more. Don't forget to shut the door. Ask, and you shall receive. Knock, and the door will open.

There is no such thing as bad weather, only unsuitable clothing. Handmade clothes lovingly made. Each piece unique. Clothe yourself with kindness, patience. They were not sugar that would melt in the rain.

Recycled trikes, painted red, lovingly restored by their dad. A simple philosophy of waste not want. Balloons tied on. Bright, simple magic too. A pop, a laugh, a silly grin. Balls made of socks; a car tire rim used for a hoop. The memory of getting a real netball between them for Christmas was a source of excitement and glee. Despite material obstacles, their mother made the representative sports teams.

She remembers this in later life. The boy down the road at

Christmas time. No food on the table, the children that Father Christmas missed. So up at four, she creeps around and hangs Santa's parcels on the door. For sometimes angels on this Earth need to help Santa, so kindness, generosity, mystery, magic, and joy remain. You never know who needs help. What goes on behind closed doors is never known.

Nip it in the bud. Instead of being the frost that kills the bud, give a flower to keep someone in the pink. Be like a boomerang of kindness and spread simple acts of kindness and love above ground. Don't judge others or show contempt. You never know when luck is down. Give someone a hand, don't look down. Help turn someone's frown upside down.

We all come into the world and go out the same way! We are all only two steps away from circumstances that can make or break us. Choose whether your experiences gift or cripple us. Don't be mean with your heart; show the power of love, the power of God within and around. The rock on solid ground. When you come to the end of your journey, ask what you have learned about yourself; what will you take from your experiences to place at the pearly gates of heaven. Have you made the world a better place? Do the inner work to create the outer gold: I love you, I'm sorry, forgive me, thank you.

So next time you pass someone homeless, sad, a little down; smile or listen for their luck may be down. Kindness paid forward makes a better place and helps the whole human race. It might be a mother who lost her husband when her son was one, or a refugee mother who lost her husband to a gun. It might be someone facing burdens all alone with a tiny ray of hope when opportunity knocks. You may be the smile or kindness that keeps them on this Earth.

A smile costs nothing. You get out of life what you put into it. Give. Fulfil someone's dreams, become a river of hope. See all children as the greatest treasure. Treat people with respect and kindness. Life comes with green light opportunities; a reminder of an attitude of gratitude for both good and bad, happy and sad, because experience shapes the way we become. Just like the diamond that started in a rock that slowly and carefully was shaped, polished to shine. We are like a diamond, so let your light shine.

We were born to make manifest the glory of God that is within us. It's not just in some of us; it's in everyone. And as we let our own light shine, we unconsciously give other people permission to do the same.
~ Marianne Williamson - *Return to Love*

Do you have the patience to polish your diamond until it shines? Biology is not your destiny, nor is your environment. 90% is attitude. The sun shines behind the clouds. Triumphs over family adversity can challenge. The old net stays in while the new net goes fishing. Stand aside, visualise, dream, aspire and of love and kindness never tire.

She leaned back on the rock and breathed, grateful for the life begun; in the sunlight, a new dawn had begun. They gave us roots and gave us wings. For the heart needs connection too. Disconnect to reconnect. Turn off the iPhone, computer too. Stop a while; don't feel blue. Look up, not down. For these two people thrived without them, and didn't land facedown.

Thank you, Mum and Dad, for your timeless gift of love and faith, in something called God—who is love—your rock. The message reiterated by Mother Theresa: T*he family that prays together stays together*; and by Martin Luther King, Jr.: *Faith is taking the first step even when you don't see the whole stair case.*

Thank you for teaching us as children to be loving, playful, and charitable, with a good work ethic; work without seeking reward, acts of kindness, give without counting the cost, the gift of giving with no expectation of return. Color the world. Help kindness grow. Create a ripple in a pool. The words, "Thank you for helping us" can turn a bad situation into a good one. Every cloud has a silver lining. Take a look at ourselves.

Thanks for being our mum – for marrying our Dad, allowing us to have wonderful sisters and brothers, a happy, secure, stable upbringing – healthy meals together around the table, working as a team and creating fun even out of boring jobs—think of the race to finish this and jobs out of a hat. Thanks for wanting the best for us all still, praying for us almost daily and your firm faith and family values. Thanks for wanting us to be happy. The good times and the bad, you are always there. We love you with all our hearts.

You made us laugh, you worked hard, and you were always there for us. We laughed, worked hard, and knew we were loved. Laughter is the best medicine you would say. The closing remarks from grandchildren are a testimony of a life well lived and loved. We admire your strength and positive attitude you consistently apply to all aspects of your life.

You have shown me how to be always positive and focus on the good things of life with your attitude. Thank you for being there with a big smile and warm hug. You are such a generous person who deserves the world.

We will forever be grateful to have such amazing grandparents like Nana and Granddad – we love you so much. Like sands through an hour glass that is the legacy of our Mum and Dad.

If there is love in the home…

If there is light in the soul, there will be beauty in the person.
If there is beauty in the person, there will be harmony in the house.
If there is harmony in the house, there will be order in the nation.
If there is order in the nation, there will be peace in the world.
~ Chinese proverb

About Julie

Julie Meates is a New Zealand-born humanitarian endeavouring to bring more peace, kindness and love into our world. Her career has been multifaceted and varied. For her, family has been important. A mother of three wonderful children and a wide, diverse, extended family.

Julie has a passion for education and health starting her early career as a teacher. She has also qualified as a social worker, counsellor and is now a barrister and solicitor, and is currently involved in post-doctoral work in education and health. She is passionate about community well-being and has worked in a volunteer capacity in many roles – with the mantra and hope that kindness may pay forward.

In 2002, she was the co-founder of *Fulfil A Dream Foundation* with a vision of strong and happy families, strong and vibrant communities and wise and visionary leadership – empowering individuals, family and communities. Fulfil A Dream Foundation was fortunate to work with high profile musicians, sportsmen, politicians, community, education and health leaders. Julie was also the chairperson of a Maori learning centre (indigenous Kohanga reo).

Currently, Julie is a volunteer with community law's programme of community justice panels. The Community Panel process aims to repair the harm caused by the offending promptly, using restorative justice processes. She has been a volunteer on United Nations executive in her Canterbury region as Board Secretary, and presently with the inception of Women of Hope Wake up, and Help Ourselves Trust Board.

She has been involved over the years with Women's Refuge and several other NGO/charitable institute non-governmental organisations – COGS (Community Organisation Grants Scheme). She was vice president of International Community Organisation (Wairarapa International Communities Incorporated) Society, and was involved in community radio doing local, national and international broadcasts. She has also worked with the homeless nationally and internationally.

Julie has been part of many community lead initiatives to strengthen communities, in sometimes complex situations, weaving together storytelling and music, and empowering youth and community talent.

She has represented sport and has coached at high school, as well as being a physical education and health teacher and tutor; and she has further qualifications in design. In her high school, she was awarded best all-round person.

Julie Meates is a quiet leader, able to inspire, influence, coordinate and empower people to achieve desired goals. Julie is experienced in working in partnership with organisations, with local communities and with individuals to make a difference. She is empathetic, positive, non-judgemental and kind, with an ability to relate to a wide range of people.

CHAPTER 13

IT'S NOT OVER
A MODEL TO LIVING THE LIFE YOU HAVE BEEN DESTINED FOR

BY PETER BLOUNT

It's no accident you are reading this. This is all ordained, as God has woven certain people into His plan. The family you were born into, where you reside—none of them are accidents to God. Failures with your spouse and children, painful experiences— none of them are accidents.

Did things not turn out the way you had hoped? Do you feel stagnant now? Do you wish you had done things differently? There are no accidents with God. God overrides our mistakes. Maybe you really blew it. You feel like your mistake has wrecked your life. Maybe you are suffering long-term consequences for a bad mistake. Remember, there are no accidents with God.

The Bible is filled with stories of people, just like you and me, that have struggled, stumbled, failed, and simply just messed up. None of us are exempt because we have all sinned and fallen short of God's glory. It's in these teachable moments that the Lord instructs us His greatest lessons, and He reveals His will along the way. It's also an opportunity to see the power of God's great mercy, forgiveness, grace, and love.

God is not the author of mistakes, and he doesn't tempt us to sin. But even when we sin and bring consequences into our lives, God in his sovereignty can even work our failures and sins for our good. In this chapter, we are focused on understanding the proper mindset to have the ability to "unearth" the "good" in our lives, and experience the life we have been waiting to live!

THE MINDSET TO UNEARTH THE GOOD

In the introduction, we addressed focusing on and understanding the proper mindset in order to have the ability to "unearth" the "good" in our lives. In order for that to take place, let's take a look at the concept.

The foundation of our growth is learning. Your teachability is instrumental in learning, and in turn, your growth. Teachability is your ability to learn by way of being taught by someone else. High teachability comes from a balance of inquiry and a willingness to learn and change. Low teachability comes from arrogance and from being a skeptic.

Learning is essential. In the Bible, there is the Master teacher, Jesus (and His Disciples); in the workforce, there are Managers (and Employees); in the school, there are Teachers (and Students); in the home, there are Parents (and Children); ... and so on. Instruction is provided in a designed manner, usually a practical method, and given with a learning goal. There is usually some form of evaluation, and if mastery is shown, there is some form of growth, progress, or promotion. That being said, open-mindedness is a major attribute needed for teachability! The ability to experience unearthing and growth lies in your teachability, where learning is the desired outcome.

Ok, now that you've determined that you're teachable and willing to learn, let's take an even closer look at the concept of unearthing. Unearthing has a spiritual connotation. Intellectual knowledge is not enough for us to gain the mindset needed to unearth. The only way that we can gain the proper mindset is by what we have termed as Faith Learning.

Trusting and clinging are important in developing the proper mindset. Faith is a mental assent to the truths AND an embracing of the truths personally by the person who assents to them. We must possess a willingness to follow the truth (even during our learning process), as this is the foundation needed for the desired freedom in our lives. This is what we call Faith Learning.

How is this done, you might ask. This is done by digging and searching for principles of truth. It begins by carefully separating the truths from the detail used to explain them, or by extracting them from an occurrence.

For example, real relationships have some fights, tears, pain, jealousy and even some insecurities which hinder growth in the relationship. However, to make them work using Faith learning, you MUST forgive as quickly as possible from the bait of Satan (staying offended and holding resentment) while putting your TRUST firmly in your only constant (God Almighty). This will require FAITH, defusing tensions, and giving patience a workout. In unearthing, there is no Plan B, the truth shall set you free!

Pray and ask for the Holy Spirit's guidance. That is the teacher needed to guide you to reveal the truth. Although there are many today who question absolute truths, too many times, truths are based on emotions. We are not to base "truth" on what we feel, how our emotions are from day-to-day. We are to base truth on what it is, God's Word. If a person is willing and open to knowing what truth is, that person will be led by the Holy Spirit to know what truth is. We should approach our quest for truth humbly and meekly to learn what it says, and to be willing to change when we are confronted with what it has to say to us.

Principles are concentrated truth, packaged for application to a wide variety of circumstances. Embracing those true principles will make decisions for oneself clear, even under the most confusing and compelling circumstances. This is saving faith and obeying actions toward those principles are what we call, unearthing.

<u>LIVING LARGE</u>

The process of unearthing is based on faith and is the application of clinging to and trusting principles of truths during any experience which embraces God as our teacher. It's the only way we can have righteousness and merit transferred to our account. Oh, to be rich in righteousness and merit—freedom, peace, and love—it's the essence of unearthing!

On the contrary, when the truth is ignored or not addressed, it hinders growth. The bait of Satan (things like ingratitude, disrespect, bitterness, not forgiving, etc.) is taken, and pride sets in! This is when one begins to feel downtrodden, doubtful, depressed, etc. They have been held captive and sent to the desert of untruths: a lonely place full of unhappiness and discontent.

Faith, then, is both a knowledge of and an assent to the facts of the Gospel, as well as a trusting, committing, or laying hold of those facts as applicable to one's own life. It is only when there is both an assent of knowledge (truths) and an embracing (clinging to) of that knowledge (truths) for oneself, that "unearthing" occurs.

Unearthing is the cornerstone to our preservation, and is the GPS (God's Preservation System) to our purpose in Him! Because even though sometimes we may find ourselves in family issues, friendship questions, marital problems, bad decisions, feelings of stagnation, depressed, lonely, etc., these are not accidents, only lessons and opportunities to practice unearthing. God overrides all of those issues by providing a GPS back to our purpose in Him.

Those experiences usually help us to define our purpose in some way and they put us in alignment with God. Our purpose will then activate passion like no other. That passion will give the freedom, peace, love, and attention that you have been desiring. However, that desire has not been placed there for you to be lauded by the world, God has placed that desire there to glorify Him! There's an old verse (John 12:32) and song that says, If I (God) be lifted up, I'll draw all men unto thee!

PAY IT FORWARD WITH INSPIRED SHARING

Potential is useless until connected properly to purpose

A subconscious action that results from unearthing is sharing. Because unearthing is spiritual, it prompts what I term as inspired sharing. Inspired sharing is whatever flows out of you that comes from the life of God within you. It's the life and energy of God manifesting itself in this physical world just as the life and energy of a vine flow into and manifests itself in fruit. Unearthing prompts inspired sharing, which in some way is tied to your purpose!

Examples of Characteristics of Inspired Sharing:

- Encouragement or wisdom.
- Thanksgiving that rises in you at a sunrise, sunset, maybe a laugh.
- Sharing in prayer.
- The paycheck you bring home, having worked unto the Lord and in love for your family and fervent service to your employer.
- The song you write, the workout you write, the song you sing, the book you read, the painting you paint, the dinner you put together to feed someone.
- The healing that comes through your prayers. (Praying for someone).
- Serving lunch at the Soup Kitchen.
- Doing chores for the elderly.

It's all the life of God in us! Don't limit him to a book. He fills the universe! With him, we can do everything, and without Him, we can do nothing. WE are merely vessels of what we are graced with. No better way to manage that new freedom and power than by sharing. The same power that enables us to unearth will be the same power that brings a desire to share.

Choose to unearth, free yourself, AND inspire others with your gifts. Otherwise, you will always feel empty, alone, depressed, unworthy, etc., and simultaneously losing yourself in purpose and life. The solution is to simply discern the principle of truth, cling, and trust Him. He is the invisible tangible life force flowing through this world and manifesting Himself visibly and tangibly THROUGH US as we glorify Him!

IN closing, let's look at the perfect example of unearthing that results in inspired sharing fueled by faith, hope, and love:

Unearthing Model:
1. Constant prayer for discernment that our principle of truth must be layered in love. We should HOPE in HIS STEADFAST LOVE (Psalm 147:11).
2. We extract the truth from our situation.
3. We should have a confident expectation(hope) of what God has promised with that truth, and its strength is in His faithfulness.
4. The hope of the righteous brings joy and peace! (Proverbs 10:28) – our freedom in life that we have been looking for!
5. Inspired Sharing (Paying it Forward): Sharing your love with a unique gift of encouragement. What we call, "Blue Clay!" (More information on this later.)

Prime Example (God):
Greater love hath no man than this, that a man lay down his life for his friends—His promise, and the ultimate in inspired sharing!

1. Constant Prayer: And GOD saw that the wickedness of man was great in the earth, and that every imagination of the thoughts of his heart was only evil continually. (Genesis 6:5 – KJV)

2. Extracted Truth: humankind's wickedness had come to the place where judgment was necessary. (Should be layered in love.)

3. Hope of what God has promised, and its strength is in its faithfulness: By faith, Noah was warned by God about things not yet seen,

4. The hope of the righteous brings joy and Peace (Noah in reverence prepared an ark for the salvation of his household, by which he condemned the world, and became an heir of the righteousness which is according to faith (Hebrews 11:7): God cleansed the world and started over.

5. Inspired Sharing: (For it is more blessed to give than to receive.) Go and bring forth fruit, and that your fruit should remain, that whatsoever ye shall ask of the Father in my name, he may give it to you. (John 15:16). For God so loved the world, that he gave his only begotten Son, that whosoever believeth in him should not perish, but have everlasting life. (John 3:16).

So, how can we remain in Christ, at peace, have a sense of freedom, and become a picture of love? If you said by unearthing, which, in essence, is obedience, then you are absolutely correct. However, there are steps we can take to become disciplined in our obedience:

1. Make sure you have a strong and firm relationship with your God. Surrounding yourself with likeminded people and putting yourself in productive environments are ways to continue your obedience and the impact that you can have on family, friends, etc. One way to do that is to join our Blue Clay Cafe, a virtual place where encouragement is the main goal daily. We have inspirational coffee study and events, among other things, to help you keep your eyes on the prize! You can join us at www.blueclaycafe.co.

2. Do not be afraid to say, "No." Do not put yourself in a position to compromise the truth. You don't have to build walls, but learn how to use boundaries. Always remind yourself of your faith and your purpose in Him. Take out your GPS, it will show you where you need to be.

3. Exercise your faith (Train) with daily devotion/study and prayer. Study to shew thyself approved unto God, a workman that needeth not to be ashamed, rightly dividing the word of truth. (2 Timothy 2:15). Meditate on Hebrews 12:11. Now, no chastening seems to be joyful for the present, but painful; nevertheless, afterward it yields the peaceable fruit of righteousness to those who have been trained by it, in the time of need.

With God as our teacher, instruction has been given (unearthing), and God puts faith to the test to prove it is genuine. As someone said, "The acid of grief tests the coin of belief." When some hardship hits in your life, your faith will be put to the test. Will you trust God? Will you lean on Him rather than lean on your own understanding? Will you become sweeter or bitter? James said, "knowing that the testing of your faith...." God tests our faith that we might know it is genuine. You should lean but never leave. Faith and grace are not earned, we don't deserve them, and we cannot merit them...it's simply our trusting and clinging to them that makes us whole. This wholeness not only allows us to be saved but to be a living example of the freedom we need, to encourage others and to glorify Him!

About Peter

Peter Blount has been a financial services field underwriter, business owner, professional athlete, teacher, coach, consultant, and speaker. He has represented the USA in a winter sport by being one of the first US athletes to set foot in East Germany after the wall came down in 1989, as well as represented the USA in a Spring Sport as a member of a team that went to Cuba (1983). It would be the first time a team had gone from the United States to Cuba since the Bay of Pigs incident in 1961!

After a lifelong series of notable achievements and honors, in 2017, he experienced a challenging three-month stretch that included a life-threatening auto accident, a divorce, and the news that his beloved mother was in the last stage of cancer. A man of Faith, he spent the next three years in transition, seeking answers. In 2020, exactly three years to the day that his tests of faith began, he received what he needed to continue the impact that was so instrumental in his previous successes.

He will now heed to the calling that he has received to impact lives with what was revealed to him during his time of transformation.

Recently, he was named to his third Hall of Fame honor and was also selected to collaborate in the writing of a book with a best-selling author.

More information and his blog can be found at:
- peterblount.com